THE BEDFORD SERIES IN HISTORY AND CULTURE

Freedom Summer

A Brief History with Documents

THE BEDFORD SERIES IN HISTORY AND CULTURE

Freedom Summer
A Brief History with Documents

John Dittmer
DePauw University

Jeffrey Kolnick
Southwest Minnesota State University

Leslie-Burl McLemore
Jackson State University

bedford/st.martin's
Macmillan Learning
Boston | New York

For Bedford/St. Martin's

Vice President, Editorial, Macmillan Learning Humanities: Edwin Hill
Publisher for History: Michael Rosenberg
Senior Executive Editor for History: William J. Lombardo
Director of Development for History: Jane Knetzger
Developmental Editor: Tess Fletcher
Editorial Assistant: Alexandra DeConti
Marketing Manager: Melissa Famiglietti
Production Editor: Lidia MacDonald-Carr
Production Coordinator: Carolyn Quimby
Director of Rights and Permissions: Hilary Newman
Permissions Associate: Michael McCarty
Permissions Manager: Kalina Ingham
Cover Design: William Boardman
Cover Photo: (Front cover) © George Ballis/Take Stock/The Image Works; (back cover, top to bottom) Amber Bowers; Rosa Tock; Frank Wilson
Project Management: Books By Design, Inc.
Cartographer: Mapping Specialists, Ltd.
Composition: Achorn International, Inc.
Printing and Binding: LSC Communications

Copyright © 2017 by Bedford/St. Martin's.

Manufactured in the United States of America.

1   0   9   8   7
f   e   d   c   b

For information, write: Bedford/St. Martin's, 75 Arlington Street, Boston, MA 02116 (617-399-4000)

ISBN 978-1-4576-6933-0

Acknowledgments

Text acknowledgments and copyrights appear at the back of the book on page 162. Art acknowledgments and copyrights appear on the same page as the text and art selections they cover; these acknowledgments and copyrights constitute an extension of the copyright page.

Foreword

The Bedford Series in History and Culture is designed so that readers can study the past as historians do.

The historian's first task is finding the evidence. Documents, letters, memoirs, interviews, pictures, movies, novels, or poems can provide facts and clues. Then the historian questions and compares the sources. There is more to do than in a courtroom, for hearsay evidence is welcome, and the historian is usually looking for answers beyond act and motive. Different views of an event may be as important as a single verdict. How a story is told may yield as much information as what it says.

Along the way the historian seeks help from other historians and perhaps from specialists in other disciplines. Finally, it is time to write, to decide on an interpretation and how to arrange the evidence for readers.

Each book in this series contains an important historical document or group of documents, each document a witness from the past and open to interpretation in different ways. The documents are combined with some element of historical narrative—an introduction or a biographical essay, for example—that provides students with an analysis of the primary source material and important background information about the world in which it was produced.

Each book in the series focuses on a specific topic within a specific historical period. Each provides a basis for lively thought and discussion about several aspects of the topic and the historian's role. Each is short enough (and inexpensive enough) to be a reasonable one-week assignment in a college course. Whether as classroom or personal reading, each book in the series provides firsthand experience of the challenge—and fun—of discovering, recreating, and interpreting the past.

Lynn Hunt
David W. Blight
Bonnie G. Smith

Preface

In the summer of 1964 in Mississippi, a coalition of civil rights organizations, operating under the umbrella of the Council of Federated Organizations (COFO), spread out into black communities across the state, challenging the Jim Crow system of segregation and all it stood for. Although activists from other parts of the country played important roles, black Mississippians were at the heart of the struggle, and local women assumed key leadership positions. Our intention in writing this book is to create a solid introduction for students to the most recent scholarship on the Mississippi summer project, or Freedom Summer as it came to be called, which serves as a microcosm of the civil rights movement as a whole.

The introduction in Part One provides a narrative account that begins with a brief history of the civil rights movement in Mississippi. It moves on to examine the recruitment of the summer volunteers, their training, and their deployment throughout the state. The summer project itself is the major focus of the introduction, which concludes with the challenge of the Mississippi Freedom Democratic Party to the "regular" state delegation at the Democratic National Convention in August in Atlantic City. Most of the participants in the summer project were of college age, and students studying this important moment in American history should be able to identify, on one level or another, with their counterparts who worked in this Deep South state more than half a century ago.

The documents in Part Two provide a window for students into the Freedom Summer movement. The first section introduces students to the movement's major program, obtaining the right to vote, and grapples with the challenges of integrating white volunteers into a civil rights coalition led by black activists. All of this was dangerous business, for most whites in the state opposed what they perceived as a threat to their way of life. Later documents focus on activists like Fannie Lou Hamer, the former sharecropper who tells of her beating in a Mississippi jail, and Dave Dennis, whose funeral oration for one of three martyred colleagues at the end of the summer was as powerful as it was anguished. Segregationists, too, have their say, in the report of the State Sovereignty Commission and in a broadside by the terrorist Ku Klux Klan. The final section of documents concerns the challenge of the new Mississippi Freedom Democratic Party to the state's all-white seg-regationist delegation at the Democratic National Convention in Atlantic City. We go behind the scenes and listen to President Lyndon Johnson in private Oval Office conversations and telephone calls, and we hear again from Fannie Lou Hamer, who testified at the convention with a national television audience hanging on her every word.

To facilitate student engagement with this history, introductory head-notes situate each document in its specific chronological context and indicate how the document speaks to larger questions. Following the documents are a chronology, questions for consideration, and a selected bibliography of key secondary sources.

Freedom Summer brought dramatic changes to the state of Missis-sippi, and its impact reverberated throughout the nation. It gave birth to the Free Speech Movement the following fall at the University of California at Berkeley, which was led by Mario Savio, who had been a summer volunteer in McComb, Mississippi. Veteran activists Casey Hayden and Mary King worked in Mississippi that summer and went on to play key roles in the movement for women's liberation. Volunteer Curtis Ganz became a top organizer in Cesar Chavez's United Farm Workers union on the West Coast. Later, gay and lesbian activists were inspired by the courageous example set by local black activists like Mrs. Hamer, as were leaders of the environmental movement. Freedom Summer, then, was the wellspring for other major movements for social justice and equality.

ACKNOWLEDGMENTS

The authors wish to thank these friends and colleagues for their wise counsel and support: Daphne Chamberlain, Pete Daniel, Michelle Deardorff, David Dennard, Jefferson Lee, Kevin Leonard, Carol Ann Madison, Tiyi Morris, Thandi Mvusi, and David Vaught. Thanks also to the reviewers, whose thoughtful and pointed comments helped make the manuscript better: Charles Bolton, University of North Carolina at Greensboro; Dennis Dickerson, Vanderbilt University; Robert Luckett, Jackson State University; Charles Payne, University of Chicago; Jason

Sokol, University of New Hampshire; and one reviewer who wishes to remain anonymous.

A special nod to Meagan Peterson, who cheerfully, expertly, and swiftly transcribed countless documents, a thankless task for which we are most thankful. And to Allen Fisher of the Lyndon Baines Johnson Presidential Library and Museum, who was of great help in making a research trip productive and was remarkably patient with later requests. We also wish to acknowledge Keith McMillian and the staff at the Fannie Lou Hamer Institute at Jackson State University.

We are also grateful to the good people at Bedford/St. Martin's, whose efforts made this book possible: Publisher Michael Rosenberg, Senior Executive Editor William Lombardo, Director of Development Jane Knetzger, Marketing Manager Melissa Famiglietti, Editorial Assistants Lexi DeConti and Arrin Kaplan, Production Editor Lidia MacDonald-Carr, Cover Designer William Boardman, and Production Coordinator Nancy Benjamin of Books By Design. And a heartfelt word of appreciation to our development editor, Tess Fletcher, whose support and encouragement sustained us along the way.

John Dittmer
Jeffrey Kolnick
Leslie-Burl McLemore

Contents

Map and Illustrations

THE BEDFORD SERIES IN HISTORY AND CULTURE

Freedom Summer

A Brief History with Documents

Introduction: Organizing for Power at the Grassroots—The Mississippi Summer Project

THE LONG BLACK FREEDOM STRUGGLE

The civil rights movement of the 1950s and 1960s was the most important social movement the United States had witnessed since the crusade to end slavery more than a century earlier. It led to passage of two monumental laws: the Civil Rights Act of 1964, which abolished discrimination in public accommodations, and the Voting Rights Act the following year, which guaranteed African Americans access to the ballot box.

This book views the black freedom struggle through a different lens. It focuses on Mississippi, reputedly the state where racism was at its worst, and on the long hot summer of 1964 when upwards of a thousand volunteers, most of them white college students, descended on the Magnolia State to participate in what would later become known as Freedom Summer. They were there to assist local black activists and their allies from outside the state in a concerted effort to crack open Mississippi's "closed society," in which white supremacy and Jim Crow segregation had reigned supreme for nearly a century.

The summer began ominously, with a confrontation in Neshoba County. On Saturday night, June 20, 1964, the White Knights of the Ku Klux Klan burned Mount Zion Methodist Church to the ground. Members of that congregation had just given civil rights workers permission to use the building for a school program that summer. The following morning, two

1

young activists from the Congress of Racial Equality (CORE) — Michael "Mickey" Schwerner, white, and James Chaney, black — drove over from Meridian to investigate. With them was Andrew Goodman, a white college student and summer volunteer from New York. Returning from Mount Zion early Sunday afternoon, the three activists were arrested by Neshoba deputy sheriff Cecil Price and taken to the county jail in Philadelphia, Mississippi. At around 10:30 p.m., the three were released, climbed into their Ford station wagon, and headed back toward Meridian. And then they vanished. (See Document 1.)

In its treatment of African Americans, Mississippi was, in the words of the NAACP's Roy Wilkins, "the worst state." Slavery had been particularly harsh in this frontier state, which was dominated by plantation owners whose word was law. The Civil War ended slavery but left much of the state in ruins. Blacks had fought for their freedom during the war, assisting the Union army as guides, spies, and combat troops, and the state's 437,000 former slaves had looked forward to full citizenship rights. During the early years of Reconstruction, black men participated in the political process for the first time, helping elect Republicans to office. These leaders rebuilt railroads and bridges in a land devastated by war, they constructed hospitals, and they established Mississippi's first public school system. Sensing that this new era of democratic promise was threatening their way of life, whites used intimidation and violence to drive blacks away from the polls in 1875, marking the end of Reconstruction and the beginning of a new era of white supremacy.

Events in the late nineteenth century established the pattern for the twentieth. Lawmakers codified racial segregation by passing a series of Jim Crow statutes, beginning with an 1888 law segregating railroad passengers. A few blacks continued to vote after the fall of Reconstruction, but that came to an end with a new state constitution in 1890 that effectively disenfranchised most African Americans for the next seventy-five years. Racial violence was a given. Between 1880 and 1940, nearly six hundred blacks were lynched in Mississippi alone, and a white man who killed a Negro had nothing to fear from a jury of his peers.

World War II brought change. Thousands of white and black Mississippians served in the military, spending time out of state and overseas. Defense industries sprang up along the Gulf Coast. Few blacks found jobs in the new factories, but the wartime labor shortages improved working conditions on the plantations and in the towns and cities. After the war, most black servicemen returning home to Mississippi tried to readjust to life in a segregated society, but a small but significant number began to think and act politically. In fact, the decade following World

War II was one of intensifying black activism, with veterans like Medgar Evers, Amzie Moore, and Aaron Henry launching voter registration campaigns as leaders of the National Association for the Advancement of Colored People (NAACP). Ten new NAACP branches in Mississippi were established between 1945 and 1947, and Evers was appointed the state's first paid NAACP field secretary in 1954, the year that the U.S. Supreme Court gave the segregationists a wake-up call.

The high court's *Brown v. Board of Education* decision, which declared segregated schools unconstitutional, did not integrate any classrooms in Mississippi, but it gave rise to the Citizens' Council, which was made up of prominent white community leaders who were determined to preserve segregation. Next the state legislature created the Sovereignty Commission, a spy agency whose major purpose was to preserve white supremacy in the Magnolia State. The following year, the U.S. Supreme Court ruled that school desegregation should proceed "with all deliberate speed." When black parents in five Mississippi cities filed desegregation petitions with their school boards, the Council crushed their efforts, usually by publicizing their names in the local newspapers. Petitioners who worked for whites lost their jobs; others were subjected to threats. Within a short time, almost all the parents had removed their names from the list.

Emboldened by the refusal of the federal government to enforce *Brown*, whites resorted to acts of violence to "keep the Negro in his place." The most shocking crime involved Emmett Till, a fourteen-year-old Chicago youth who traveled down to Mississippi to visit his uncle. While hanging out with a group of boys in the hamlet of Money, Till went into a grocery store and allegedly whistled at a white woman. For this, her husband and his half-brother abducted the young man, shot him, tied his body to a cotton gin fan, and dumped it in the Tallahatchie River. The two men were tried, but a jury quickly found them innocent. A year later, for money, they told a *Look* magazine reporter that yes, they had murdered Emmett Till. (See Document 2.)

The Till lynching had a devastating effect on civil rights activity in Mississippi. Once-flourishing NAACP branches now struggled to survive. A courageous Medgar Evers crisscrossed the state, month after month, encouraging frightened NAACP members. But it would take events occurring outside Mississippi to bring the movement there back to life.

First there was the sit-in movement in 1960, which spread across the upper South, followed a year later by the freedom rides, whose goal was to desegregate bus and train terminals. That summer, hundreds of freedom riders did time in Mississippi's notorious Parchman Penitentiary.

Out of the sit-ins and freedom rides there emerged a new organization, the Student Nonviolent Coordinating Committee (SNCC, pronounced "Snick"). Unlike older groups like the NAACP and Martin Luther King's Southern Christian Leadership Conference (SCLC), which relied on educated ministers and professionals to provide leadership, SNCC sought out maids, sharecroppers, independent farmers, and small business entrepreneurs.

This revolutionary approach, in which ordinary citizens participated in the planning and implementation of all programs, received its baptism of fire in the southwest Mississippi town of McComb. Led by Bob Moses, a New York schoolteacher who would achieve legendary status in the civil rights movement, SNCC activists launched a voter registration campaign in McComb in the summer and fall of 1961. The Mississippi voter registration process was complicated, designed so that the registrar could deny blacks their right to vote. (See Document 3.) Once they became aware of the challenge to their supremacy, McComb police, elected officials, and ordinary white citizens targeted the young organizers, initiating a campaign of intimidation and violence that included the murder of local activist Herbert Lee. SNCC workers retreated, leaving McComb until the summer of 1964, but they had learned valuable lessons there that they applied in their future campaigns throughout Mississippi and the Deep South (see map).

Early in 1962, Moses met with leaders from CORE, SCLC, and state and local NAACP branches to form the Council of Federated Organizations (COFO). (See Document 4.) Mississippi was the only state where all the civil rights organizations operated under the same banner. SNCC initiated its first project as part of COFO in Greenwood in the Delta. Unlike the mobilization campaigns led by Dr. King, which featured demonstrations and demands for desegregation of public facilities, SNCC chose voter registration, in part because unlike sit-ins and picketing, it was a program all blacks could identify with. In addition, it provided the best opportunity to develop local leaders who would carry on the struggle long after the SNCC workers moved on. Led at first by two young black Mississippians, Sam Block and Willie Peacock, the Greenwood movement developed slowly, but it eventually made inroads by first attracting teenagers to the cause, and then their parents. In Greenwood, entire families became involved. And beginning with the Delta campaign, women entered the movement in large numbers, participating in all phases of activity. Historian Charles Payne found that in the Delta, and in the rural South generally, women were in fact much more politically active than men. (See Document 5.) SNCC was searching

Mississippi with Areas of Civil Rights Activity, Summer 1964

for nontraditional sources of leadership, and women represented an enormous pool of untapped potential. Inspired by the courage of local women who ran great risks by attempting to register, civil rights activists began to make inroads in the local black community, and the voting rights campaign picked up steam. (See Document 6.)

Greenwood attracted national attention when SNCC activist Jimmy Travis was shot and seriously wounded. But when the administration of President John Kennedy backed away from a pledge to protect those attempting to register, the movement in the Delta declined for a time. The Kennedy administration made it clear that except in extreme cases, as when James Meredith desegregated the University of Mississippi in the fall of 1962, it would not protect civil rights workers attempting to exercise their constitutional rights. It was the responsibility of local and state government officials to enforce the laws. (See Document 7.) Without the threat of federal intervention, police and other local whites terrorized and intimidated Delta residents. The same fate awaited activists in other parts of the state.

Down in Jackson, a student-led boycott of downtown merchants was stopped in its tracks after the assassination of NAACP leader Medgar Evers in June 1963. That same week, a group of black women returning from an SCLC leadership school decided to integrate the white waiting room at the bus station in Winona. For this, they were arrested, thrown in jail, and brutally beaten. One of those women, Fannie Lou Hamer, would tell her story to a national television audience a year later. (See Document 8.) In Clarksdale, where state NAACP president Aaron Henry had built a broad-based local movement, whites simply drew the line, refused to negotiate with black leaders, and kept the jails full of demonstrators. Determined to keep their movement alive, Mississippi activists concluded that a change in tactics was necessary.

The new strategy took shape in the summer of 1963 with a COFO decision to hold a statewide mock (unofficial) election. The purpose of this "freedom vote" was to dramatize black disenfranchisement and to expand the movement into new areas. Organizers also hoped the campaign would generate national publicity and force the federal government to intervene in Mississippi. COFO nominated NAACP state president Aaron Henry for governor and Ed King, a native white Mississippian and chaplain at historically black Tougaloo College, for lieutenant governor. To get out a large vote, SNCC sent all available staff to Mississippi. They were assisted in the campaign's final weeks by nearly a hundred white students from Yale and Stanford, recruited by a charismatic white activist named Allard Lowenstein. Their presence was duly noted. More than eighty-three thousand blacks cast their ballots, an impressive turnout. A closer look at the vote, however, reveals the difficult problems that lay ahead. Two-thirds of the total vote came from just eight counties, and twenty-five of the state's eighty-two counties reported fewer than one hundred votes each. After the freedom ballots were counted, Bob Moses concluded that "the Negroes of Mississippi will not get the vote until the equivalent of an army is sent here." Organizers were also disappointed that the national media did not pay much attention to the election, and the coverage focused mainly on the white volunteers from Yale and Stanford.

ORGANIZING FREEDOM SUMMER

Three weeks after the freedom vote, President Kennedy was assassinated in Dallas. Although movement activists knew he was no civil rights hero, they mourned his death and were apprehensive about his successor, Lyndon Johnson, a southerner. In the days and weeks following the assassination, movement activity declined across the South. In Mississippi, COFO leaders faced a dilemma: should they return to low-key, grassroots organizing in individual communities, or should they build on the foundation laid by the freedom vote and initiate another ambitious statewide campaign?

White supremacists in Mississippi were also rethinking their strategy. For the past decade, the Citizens' Council had been the guardian of the color line, succeeding in preventing blacks from mounting serious challenges to a Jim Crow system in place for nearly a century. But the business and professional men who ran the Council had not destroyed the movement, and their failure led directly to the rebirth of the Ku Klux Klan. Although racist violence against blacks had been steadily increasing since the *Brown* decision, the Klan as an organization had faded away since its first revival in the 1920s. But now it appeared to hard-core racists that only a reign of terror could preserve the southern way of life. In December 1963, a month after the freedom vote, the White Knights of the Ku Klux Klan in Mississippi organized in Natchez and spread rapidly across the countryside. Throughout the winter and spring of 1964, night riders roamed the state. On a single night in May, the Klan burned crosses in sixty-four counties. Black homes, businesses, and churches were bombed and burned. (See Document 9.) Mississippi officials and police did nothing to deter the violence—in some cases, the police *were* the Klan—and President Johnson appeared to be following the same hands-off policy as his predecessor.

This new threat lent a sense of urgency. With the Klan running wild, how could COFO persuade local people to come to a meeting, much less go down to the courthouse and, in full view of the public, try to register to vote? What would it take to convince federal officials that they needed to protect human rights in the Deep South? Why not do something really dramatic, like inviting not a hundred but a thousand college students to spend their summer vacation working in Mississippi? These volunteers would be assigned to projects across the state, assisting with voter registration, helping set up community centers, and teaching in the new freedom schools, which would represent a bold departure from Mississippi's traditional educational system.

The most contentious issue facing COFO was not the idea of a summer project, but the relative merit of bringing down hundreds of white college students. (See Document 10.) From its inception, SNCC had been an interracial organization. A handful of whites had worked in Mississippi. But most SNCC field secretaries opposed bringing in large numbers of them. An expanded white presence, they argued, would divert resources away from the primary mission of organizing and empowering black communities. Putting white faces in black neighborhoods could also increase the likelihood of Klan violence, particularly if white female volunteers were seen with black men. Moreover, with the confidence that came with money and education, university students could intimidate and embarrass local blacks. (See Document 11.)

Those favoring a large white presence included COFO leaders Bob Moses and Dave Dennis and black Mississippians like Fannie Lou Hamer, who argued at a heated COFO meeting in November that "if we're trying to break down this barrier of segregation, we can't segregate ourselves." The major argument, however, was pragmatic: Unless America was awakened to what was going down in the Magnolia State, white Mississippians would continue to employ terrorist tactics to destroy the movement. So long as it was black people who were being brutalized, white Americans paid little attention. White students, on the other hand, would bring with them visibility and publicity, and their presence might force a reluctant federal government to protect them and other civil rights workers in the exercise of their First Amendment rights.

The debate over bringing in large numbers of volunteers continued throughout the fall and early winter. Characteristically, Moses did not push his point of view, even when these discussions dragged on into the next year. (See Document 12.) All that changed, however, when he learned of the murder of Louis Allen in February 1964. Allen's "crime" was that he had witnessed the murder of voter registration worker Herbert Lee in southwest Mississippi in 1961 and then told the FBI what he saw. From that point on, he was a marked man. As the threats mounted, he decided to leave the state. The day before his departure, he was gunned down on his front lawn. No one was charged with his murder. From this, Moses concluded, "We were just defenseless, there was no way to bring national attention. And it seemed to me like we were just sitting ducks. People were just going to be wiped out." Moses won over the doubters, and the recruiting effort on northern campuses began in earnest, with Friends of SNCC chapters in the North playing a key role in interviewing potential volunteers. (See Documents 13–16.)

At the end of the recruiting drive, COFO invited the volunteers to one of two orientation meetings at the Western College for Women in Oxford, Ohio. The first session, June 14–20, was designed for those who would be doing voter registration, and the second centered around training teachers for the new freedom schools and staff for the community centers. Two hundred and fifty volunteers attended the first session, and some three hundred young people arrived a week later. They would be joined in Mississippi by other college students who were unable to attend either session at Oxford and by volunteer lawyers, doctors, nurses, and social workers. There may have been close to a thousand volunteers in Mississippi that summer, but no more than six hundred were in the state at any one time. More than 40 percent of the applicants were women. Blacks made up only about 10 percent of the volunteer contingent.

Several factors account for the relatively low turnout of African American volunteers. Colleges were the major recruiting ground, and only 3 percent of all undergraduates were black. Moreover, most black students needed to work during the summers to help finance their education. And some northern blacks were no doubt deterred by their parents, many of whom knew southern racism firsthand and did not want their children put in harm's way.

Most of the first batch of volunteers had just finished their final exams and arrived in Oxford full of enthusiasm. Their "teachers" were the embattled SNCC veterans, many of whom had been in the field for nearly three years. They were not in a festive mood, and from the outset they worried that the eager faces at the meeting would not be prepared for what white Mississippi had in store for them. Moses told SNCC staff

Figure 1. *Freedom Summer Volunteers at Oxford, Ohio, Orientation, June 1964*
Movement activists assumed that some volunteers would be assaulted in Mississippi. Here, COFO staff members are showing the volunteers how to protect themselves, nonviolently, when attacked.

Herbert Randall Photograph, McCain Library and Archives, The University of Southern Mississippi.

members that they "must try to set a tone so that the summer volunteers can understand problems the staff has and understand what they are getting into, who they're working with." This was a difficult task to accomplish in only one week. (See Figure 1 and Document 17.)

From the outset, the two groups danced around each other, with the volunteers growing increasingly concerned that their hosts disliked them and did not want to be with them in Mississippi. Things came to a head over a CBS television documentary, *Mississippi and the Fifteenth Amendment.* The volunteers watched attentively as an obese registrar with a heavy southern drawl explained why Negroes did not really want to vote, but then they burst into laughter: The man and his message were ludicrous. SNCC and CORE workers were watching a very different program. The registrar was Theron Lynd, a powerful symbol of white repression; he had humiliated hundreds of blacks who, at great personal risk, had attempted to register and vote. Several members of the Mississippi staff walked out of the meeting in disgust, and those who remained tore into the volunteers for their behavior. Fighting back tears, one organizer concluded, "I hope by the end of the summer you will never laugh at such a film again." Later that night, staff members and volunteers held an informal meeting where both sides spoke their minds. Black-white relations within the movement varied from project to project, but interracial tensions lay near the surface throughout the summer.

On Saturday, June 20, the first group of volunteers boarded buses and cars to make the long trip south to the Magnolia State. It was, one volunteer noted, "a strange combination of children headed for summer camp and soldiers going off to war." One of the volunteers, New Yorker Andy Goodman, rode down with Mickey Schwerner and James Chaney. Their destination was the relatively safe CORE project in Meridian.

The next day, the second wave of volunteers arrived in Oxford. On Monday morning, Bob Moses received word that three civil rights workers had been missing for twenty-four hours, and he called the volunteers together to tell them the news. The disappearance of Chaney, Schwerner, and Goodman had a sobering effect on both the volunteers and the COFO staff. One volunteer recalled that the mood on the campus was "like a funeral parlor." SNCC activist Judy Richardson noted that each morning, Bob Moses walked "slowly to the blackboard on the stage in the auditorium and, without saying a word, wrote 'The three are still missing.' Just those words. Nothing else." At the end of the week, before the volunteers boarded the buses, Moses told them he had concluded that "the kids are dead."

Many white Mississippians persuaded themselves that the whole story of the missing civil rights workers was a hoax. Senator James Eastland called it "a publicity stunt." Others speculated that the three were in Cuba, enjoying the hospitality of Fidel Castro. Two days after their disappearance, however, FBI agents searching the area found a badly burned blue Ford station wagon owned by Schwerner. Local whites were still not convinced, believing that COFO must have burned their own car to make the hoax look convincing. Under pressure, President Johnson persuaded FBI director J. Edgar Hoover to beef up the agency's presence in Mississippi and sent former CIA director Allen Dulles to Jackson to investigate. (See Documents 18–20.)

As the nation's attention focused on the events in Neshoba County, the summer project got under way. Volunteers moved into each of the thirty-two COFO projects scattered across the state. Most were in SNCC territory, but CORE had the responsibility for the Fourth Congressional District, which included Meridian and Canton. The Gulf Coast, which depended on the tourist trade, was a relatively safe area. There COFO initiated the White Folks Project, in which a group of white activists sought—with limited success—to establish a beachhead in the local white community. The larger projects, such as the one in Hattiesburg, had more than forty volunteers in residence, while the smaller ones were staffed by as few as two.

There was another contingent of summer volunteers whose contributions have been overshadowed by all the attention paid to the northern students. Lawyers, doctors, and ministers came into the state, usually for short periods of time, making their professional services available to the civil rights workers. The most controversial agency of "adult" volunteers was the National Lawyers Guild, a group of left-wing attorneys who had long championed civil rights but had also represented alleged Communists during the Red Scare of the McCarthy era of the late 1940s and 1950s. COFO welcomed the group's legal assistance, refusing to resort to red-baiting. The NAACP Legal Defense Fund also sent lawyers to Mississippi that summer to provide counsel to civil rights workers persecuted by white legal authorities.

The National Council of Churches (NCC) enthusiastically supported the summer project, sponsoring a minister-counselor program that eventually drew approximately 275 clergy and laypeople from all over the country. Most came for ten days to two weeks. They provided spiritual guidance to the volunteers and, equally important, listened sympathetically to young people who were attempting to cope in a hostile environment. The NCC's commitment to Mississippi lasted beyond the summer. It created an agency, the Delta Ministry, that provided valuable assistance to the civil rights forces in years to come.

Early on it became clear that the volunteers might need medical attention for problems related to stress as well as for the normal ailments afflicting young people moving into a new and strange environment. Few of the state's white doctors would have anything to do with these activists, and of the fifty-some black physicians, only a handful would treat civil rights workers. Responding to the need, a group of health care professionals from New York joined local black doctors to form the Medical Committee for Human Rights. Nearly a hundred health care professionals spent a week or two in Mississippi. They treated volunteers and veteran activists afflicted by minor medical ailments, and they counseled veteran activists suffering from "battle fatigue," later diagnosed as post-traumatic stress disorder. Psychologist Robert Coles spent time in Mississippi and observed that "in many ways these young civil rights workers are in a war and exposed to the stresses of warfare."

For many white Mississippians, the influx of hundreds of integrationists constituted an "invasion" that had to be repelled. During its spring session, the state legislature passed a series of laws banning picketing and leafleting, while doubling the number of state police. Jackson's mayor, Alan Thompson, also greatly increased the size of his force, bought two hundred shotguns and ordered fifty more, converted two city trucks into troop carriers, and purchased a combat vehicle (which became known as Thompson's Tank) that carried ten officers and two drivers, with shotguns protruding from gunports. Rumors spread like wildfire. Some whites were convinced, for example, that black men sporting white bandages around their necks had been designated to rape white women. Gun and ammunition sales and Klan memberships boomed. In McComb, local whites founded Help, Inc., a self-defense group organized in a middle-class white neighborhood. Members set up an alarm system to warn of an imminent attack by the civil rights workers. Help, Inc., guidelines warned citizens to "keep inside during darkness or during periods of threats. Know where your children are at all times. . . . Do not stand by and let your neighbor be assaulted."

Given this level of paranoia, it is not surprising that the summer of 1964 was the most violent in Mississippi since Reconstruction. Before the summer ended, there were at least six racial murders, thirty-five shooting incidents, and sixty-five homes and other buildings bombed, including thirty-five churches. One thousand movement people were arrested, and eighty activists suffered beatings. Most of the physical violence was directed against local blacks and veteran civil rights activists.

Shocked and sickened by the terrorist attacks directed against the black community, COFO staff members nonetheless pushed ahead with their program. SNCC had offices in thirteen communities in the Delta. CORE's sites in the Fourth Congressional District included major projects in Canton and Meridian. Thanks to the added volunteer manpower, COFO established bases in twelve more communities by the end of the summer.

Most of the young volunteers stayed with local black families, paying them a modest ten dollars a week for room and board. In addition to providing food and lodging, the hosts took a personal interest in the health and safety of their guests. These families were the unsung heroes of the movement. The summer project could not have gotten off the ground without them, and they knew that they risked retaliation from local whites for housing these young people. As volunteer and artist Tracy Sugarman put it, "Everybody knew that we were going home at the end of the summer. The people that took us in were gonna stay. So they were there for the reprisals, for the anger that the white community had to bring to bear on 'em." Friendships often lasted long beyond the summer, with a number of the "adopted" volunteers returning to visit their "families" in the years that followed.

The volunteers needed all the support they could get from the black community, because the environment outside was hostile. (See Document 21.) Civil rights workers were subject to attack by whites and arrest by the police. Project directors told volunteers not to drink alcohol, curse in public, or go out at night. Interracial dating was forbidden in some projects and discouraged elsewhere. White volunteer Karen Kunstler recalls being jailed and asked a lot of questions by the sheriff, who "wanted me to describe the size of black men's penises. They were obsessed with sex. I don't think we were obsessed with sex. But it was a clear message that that's all they thought we were doing."

COMMUNITY CENTERS AND FREEDOM SCHOOLS

The new recruits were put to work immediately in all the projects. Some volunteers (mostly women) were assigned to the community centers, many of which were just getting started. The nascent community centers were designed to create public spaces for the local black community where they could conduct classes, organize for political purposes, or set up medical clinics. Often the community centers were repurposed buildings, and few new centers were completed. The idea behind them was consistent with all of the thinking behind the summer project—to build for the black community what was considered commonplace in the white community. Much more successful were the freedom schools, an educational experiment made necessary by the shortcomings of the public schools.

Although it was the poorest state in the Union, Mississippi had maintained two different school systems since the end of the Civil War. Under the doctrine of "separate but equal," white children were the beneficiaries of the meager funds available to support the schools. Their needs always took priority: Their school year was nearly two months longer, their buildings were better and had libraries, while most black schools did not. Whites received free bus transportation. Many black students had none. In those districts where buses were available, black students often had to pay for the privilege. It is not surprising, then, that as late as 1950 seven blacks in ten had less than a seventh-grade education, and only 2.3 percent had completed high school.

Because all the schools, black and white, were under the control of white school boards, black teachers knew they had to toe the line on racial issues or risk losing their jobs. In most school districts, African American history and contemporary race relations were taboo subjects. One freedom school teacher in Hattiesburg reported that in her class of teenagers not one had heard about the *Brown* decision. Another observed that "the only thing that our kids knew about Negro history was Booker T. Washington and George Washington Carver and his peanuts." There were outstanding black educators across the state who opened the world to their students and taught them their rights as citizens. But these teachers were exceptional, and the organizers of the freedom schools knew their major responsibility was to "fill an artistic and creative vacuum in the lives of Negro Mississippians and to get them to articulate their own desires, demands, and questions." (See Document 22.)

The freedom schools were the brainchild of SNCC veteran Charlie Cobb. His "Prospectus for a Summer Freedom School Program" called for a comprehensive program. Traditional academic subjects composed a significant part of the curriculum, but it also included a strong political component. A primary goal of the freedom schools was to "form the basis for statewide student action."

Teachers across the country had been accustomed to spoon-feeding their students in classrooms where law and order was the rule. Educator Florence Howe taught that summer in Jackson and later wrote that the teacher in the freedom school was not to be "an omnipotent, aristocratic dictator, a substitute for the domineering parent or the paternalistic state. . . . The freedom school teacher is in fact to be present not simply to teach, but to learn with the students." The curriculum combined remedial work in traditional subjects like reading, writing, and math, but it also included a variety of specialized classes in such areas as foreign language, science, dance, and debate, depending on the interests and expertise of the teacher. Under the heading "Leadership Development," each school offered a series of courses on the history and philosophy of the civil rights movement, current events, and "Negro" history. As for the teachers, most were white women. COFO organizers were concerned about the safety of these volunteers, and teaching in a freedom school was not as dangerous as doing voter registration work on a plantation. Moreover, because teaching was a profession dominated by women, it seemed natural at that time to put female volunteers in the classroom. Most, though, had no teaching experience.

By summer's end, upwards of twenty-five hundred students were attending some forty schools across the state. Enrollment varied from school to school. Jackson, Canton, and Meridian each had more than a hundred enrollees. Hattiesburg became "the mecca of the freedom school world," with six hundred students enrolled at several sites.

The freedom schools, then, were an enormous success. Letters home from teachers were enthusiastic. Pamela Parker, from Bucks County, Pennsylvania, wrote her parents that "the atmosphere in class is unbelievable. It is what every teacher dreams about—real, honest enthusiasm and desire to learn anything and everything." Activist historian Howard Zinn visited a number of schools and reported that while it was difficult to point to concrete results, "nine year-old Negro children sounded out French words whose English equivalents they had not yet discovered. . . . They learned about Frederick Douglass, wrote letters to the local editor about segregation, and discussed the meaning of civil disobedience. Some wrote short stories about their lives, and others wrote poems." (See Document 23.) Students heard Pete Seeger sing songs from Africa, India, and China; they listened while the veteran labor organizer and activist A. Philip Randolph talked about his life in the struggle; and they attended plays put on by the Free Southern Theatre, which had recently organized in Mississippi and was performing in towns and hamlets across the state.

Although at the time COFO veterans did not accord high status to the schools—the "real work," after all, was registering black voters—in the long run the freedom schools stand out as one of the summer's major achievements. They opened new worlds to several thousand black youngsters, enhancing their self-esteem and raising their expectations. They proved that a creative, student-centered, anti-authoritarian approach to teaching and learning had, and still has, much to offer the tradition-bound educational establishment, both in Mississippi and throughout the nation. (See Document 24.)

The freedom school teachers and their students were both witnesses to and participants in the dramatic events occurring throughout the Magnolia State. The search for the missing civil rights workers continued without result, despite a massive federal presence that included a greatly expanded FBI regional office in Jackson. In mid-July, the bodies of two young black men in their early twenties were discovered in a bayou near the Mississippi River. Charles Moore and Henry Dee had been abducted by Klansmen, who bound them to a tree and beat them to death. Although the FBI arrested two men, the state refused to prosecute, claiming insufficient evidence. Later, the body of a black teenager, never identified, was found floating in the Black River, wearing a CORE T-shirt. Once it was clear that these were not the missing civil rights workers, the press and the public lost interest. (See Document 25.)

While acts of violence were common throughout the state, they were pervasive in the Delta. SNCC had moved its national office from Atlanta to Greenwood for the summer to take advantage of the large base of support it had developed in the Delta over the past two years. This was an area where local people, especially the youth, were now eager to confront the white establishment, and it was the job of Stokely Carmichael to calm them down. Born in the West Indies, the twenty-two-year-old SNCC field secretary and Howard University graduate had been named coordinator of the Second Congressional District, which encompassed the Delta. Flamboyant and charismatic, Carmichael was also a disciplined organizer who insisted that the civil rights workers in his jurisdiction keep a low profile: "We're not here to go to jail. We're here to do a job. Which cannot be done in a cell." (See Figure 2.)

He thought he had succeeded in persuading young people that the time was not right, that too much was at stake in the summer project to provoke what was certain to be a violent white response in defense of Jim Crow. But in early July, Congress passed the Civil Rights Act, which outlawed racial discrimination in public accommodations. And then a delegation from the national office of the NAACP, led by Director of Branches Gloster Current, came to Mississippi to test the new law.

National NAACP officers, including Current and Roy Wilkins, had viewed Freedom Summer unfavorably, and as a result, the national media were not paying them much attention. Here was an opportunity to grab the spotlight. A nine-member, integrated delegation flew into Jackson on July 5 and registered at the Heidelberg, the city's most prestigious hotel, where the manager greeted them "with a smile." The story made the front page of the *New York Times*. The following day, a three-car caravan headed out to test facilities in other cities, including Greenwood. There, "with their press and FBI entourage, of course they got served," said Carmichael, and "then they split as fast as their cars would take them." Returning to New York, Current wrote that "other citizens must be encouraged to take advantage of the facilities throughout the state at every opportunity."

Figure 2. *Stokely Carmichael, under Arrest in Mileston, Summer 1964*
Although Carmichael had warned the summer volunteers to avoid situations where they might be arrested, this proved impossible, even for a seasoned activist like Carmichael.
1976 Matt Herron / Take Stock / The Image Works.

In Greenwood, Silas McGhee had already done just that. On July 5, the day that the NAACP delegation landed in Jackson, the Greenwood teenager decided to see a movie at the all-white LeFlore theater. He bought a ticket, walked in, and sat down. Soon whites began pelting him with paper and trash. He complained to the manager, who refused to intervene. McGhee returned to his seat, only to be jumped by more than a dozen white men. Fleeing the theater, he went directly to the police station. The officer at the desk asked, "Who put you up to this?" McGhee told him, "I only wanted to see a movie."

Silas was not involved in the Greenwood movement at the time, but his family had long been active. The McGhees were typical in that often entire families committed to the movement, setting a positive example for those who were reluctant to participate. Silas's older brother Jake worked with SNCC. Clarence Robinson, his half-brother, was a career army man who spent his furlough time in Greenwood. Volunteer and author Sally Belfrage remembers him as "a six-foot six paratrooper with a thirty-six-inch reach and a 136 IQ. . . . He walked down the street in his uniform like Wild Bill Hickok on the way to a duel, cool, tough, infinitely menacing." Their mother, Laura McGhee, had been among the first local blacks to open their doors to the movement, inviting SNCC workers to hold rallies at her fifty-eight-acre farm. She gained notoriety later in the summer when, after two police officers harassed her and a third hit her in the chest, Mrs. McGhee countered with a right punch to his jaw, staggering the policeman, and then calmly walked away.

It soon became clear to Carmichael and other COFO leaders that it was impossible to carry out their mission for the summer and avoid confrontation with local whites, for doing the job often meant getting arrested. This first became apparent in mid-July, when Greenwood blacks held a "Freedom Day." Scores of local people marched to the courthouse to attempt to register, overcoming their fears and taking a stand. A number of the participants carried picket signs in defiance of a new state law forbidding them. One hundred and eleven Greenwood blacks, SNCC field secretaries, and summer volunteers were arrested for picketing and filled three jails. That night hundreds more attended the largest mass meeting in the history of the local movement. (See Figure 3.)

It needs to be noted, however, that at no point did a majority of black Mississippians actively support the freedom struggle. As they made their rounds, civil rights workers frequently met with indifference that masked real fears. When they canvassed a neighborhood, knocking on doors, many residents either pretended they were not home, made excuses, or promised to go to the courthouse to register but did not show up. Participating in a demonstration took even more courage than confronting the county registrar. Charles McLaurin was in that first wave of SNCC field secretaries to move into the Delta. His territory included Ruleville, and he became one of Fannie Lou Hamer's closest friends. When McLaurin attempted to organize a registration drive in Drew, a small town north of Ruleville, police arrested seven people for distributing literature without a permit. The following day, the pastor of a black church withdrew permission for a meeting. McLaurin then led a group of blacks onto the sidewalk for an impromptu rally. Police looked on, as did a group of black men across the street. McLaurin urged the men to join the group. When they failed to respond, the frustrated SNCC field secretary shouted, "Are you gonna let them see that you're afraid? That you won't join these kids and women?" No one moved, except the police, who arrested twenty-five demonstrators for blocking the sidewalk. This pattern of breakthroughs and setbacks, of defiant courage and sullen resignation, coexisted in projects across the state.

Figure 3. *Mass Meeting in McComb, Summer 1964*
COFO returned to McComb during Freedom Summer. Here Project Director
Curtis Hayes (*center*) is leading a group of townspeople and volunteers in the
movement anthem, "We Shall Overcome," prior to marching to the courthouse
for a "Freedom Day" event, where local people would attempt to register to
vote.
1976 George Ballis / Take Stock / The Image Works.

For the Freedom Summer volunteers, a week's orientation in Ohio
did not prepare them for confrontations with Mississippi whites or
for life inside the project. The reservations expressed by a number of
SNCC field secretaries in the spring, that volunteers from prestigious
northern universities—arrogant, confident, and naive—would come
down and try to assume leadership positions, were borne out in a few
cases. Perhaps the most notorious example occurred in the Vicksburg
project, where white volunteer Paul Cowan was given the job of communications officer. In his candid account of his summer in Mississippi,
Cowan recalled that he became impatient with what he perceived as the
autocratic leadership of the project director, a twenty-two-year-old black
man who had dropped out of college. Along with several other volunteers, Cowan intimidated the SNCC veteran to the point where he spent
less and less time in the COFO office. Cowan founded a movement
newspaper, the *Vicksburg Citizen's Appeal*, insisting that it be indepen-
dently operated. He was shocked and angered, then, when Bob Moses

came over to Vicksburg, voiced strong support for the project director, and told Cowan that the paper must be accountable to COFO. Years later, Cowan ruefully reflected that "we were so intent on transforming Mississippi in a summer that we were unable to relate to its people as human beings. . . . There is a kind of Jesus Christ complex that many middle-class whites bring to their relations with people whom they consider oppressed."

A concern in some of the projects was interracial sex, particularly relationships between black male civil rights workers and white female volunteers. Local blacks frowned on this behavior, black women resented it, and segregationists became enraged at the mere sighting of an interracial couple. These liaisons could create serious problems, and project directors tried to discourage them. As SNCC veteran Ivanhoe Donaldson put it, such activity would "provide local whites with the initiative they need to come in here and kill all of us." The extent of sexual activity between blacks and whites that summer has no doubt been exaggerated, in part because white supremacists had made it a centerpiece of their attack on the summer project itself. Still, in a number of projects some white female volunteers did have sex with black men, who at times came on aggressively. White SNCC worker Mary King, also in Mississippi that summer, later wrote that "sexual dalliances were one way for a volunteer to prove that she was not racist, and I'm sure any number of black men manipulated this anxiety." Viewed politically, such activity caused internal problems in the projects and weakened the links between COFO and local black communities.

An obvious but important point to remember is that the volunteers came to Mississippi because they had been invited. They wanted to become part of the movement. In so doing, they assumed risks, and some, like Frances O'Brien, paid for their idealism. A native of Southern California, twenty-one-year-old Fran O'Brien was assigned to Vicksburg, considered relatively safe by Mississippi standards. She taught in a freedom school and was "delighted" with the work being done by her pupils. Later in the summer, she and five other volunteers walked from the Vicksburg Freedom Center to the end of a long driveway, waiting to be picked up and taken home to their host families. The car that pulled up could only hold five passengers, and the driver was unwilling to risk arrest for overcrowding. He assured Fran that another SNCC car was on the way, and "sure enough, there it was." She ran over to the stopped vehicle, only to discover four men wearing white hoods inside. Apparently on their way to a Klan meeting, they assumed she was a civil rights worker, dragged her into the car, and drove to a deserted field, no doubt pleased at their good fortune, "capturing a little nigger-lover like that without even the trouble of hunting." As the driver ordered her out of the car, another Klansman took two pieces of rubber hose out of the trunk and commanded her to "bend over the hood and don't try any funny business." One of the men yanked up her skirt, she said later, and then "the Klansmen took turns, two of them beating until they were tired, then passing on their hoses to the other two. Each blow stung harder than the one before. After what seemed a long time the pain began to grow duller. . . . The next thing I knew I was lying on the ground in the driveway of the Freedom Center." Fran O'Brien was so traumatized by the Klan attack that she could not tell her comrades about it. In fact, she did not speak of the incident to anyone for the next fifteen years.

It is difficult to generalize about the impact of the summer volunteers. Along with other factors, their presence did push the Mississippi movement in a new direction, one that relied increasingly on focusing the national spotlight on the Magnolia State. As for the summer itself, for the most part, "they did just fine," observed Stokely Carmichael. Civil rights scholar Doug McAdam's conclusion that "they were tried and not found wanting" applies to the vast majority of the students, clergy, lawyers, and doctors who made up the volunteer brigade in the summer of 1964. (See Document 26.)

DEMANDING THE RIGHT TO VOTE

On July 19, Bob Moses sent out a memorandum to all COFO project staff members, stating that "*everyone* who is not working on Freedom Schools or community centers *must* devote all their time to organizing for the convention challenge." (See Document 27.) COFO had founded the Mississippi Freedom Democratic Party (MFDP) in the spring with the intent of challenging the legitimacy of the all-white, segregationist state delegation at the Democratic National Convention in Atlantic City in late August. Now time was running out, and only twenty-one thousand people had signed up as members. Such a low registration figure would undermine the challenge's credibility.

Voter registration had been the heart and soul of the SNCC program in Mississippi for nearly three years, but with minimal tangible result. Although several thousand blacks had risked their jobs (and their dignity) to make the trip to the courthouse to take the test, few had succeeded in passing. The test was rigged against them, and the county registrar, often an intimidating presence, alone determined whether the applicant had answered the questions correctly. Moreover, the local newspaper published the names of those attempting to register, leaving the applicants vulnerable to economic retaliation. It is not surprising, then, that when the summer volunteers went door to door asking people to take the time to go to the courthouse, they were often rebuffed. One discouraged volunteer wrote home, "Canvassing is dirty work. It is very tiring, and frankly boring after the first hour or so. It is almost impossible to overcome the fears."

So with only a month remaining before the start of the national convention, COFO shifted its focus from voter registration to MFDP recruitment. Movement workers now fanned out into the countryside and canvassed in pool halls, barbershops, and beauty parlors in the towns and cities, making the point that in signing up with the party, blacks were not at risk: Their names would not appear in the newspaper, and they would not lose their jobs. While some local people remained fearful, the last-ditch registration campaign bore positive results. By convention time, eighty thousand African Americans and a few white supporters had become card-carrying members of the Mississippi Freedom Democratic Party.

To mount a successful challenge, the MFDP needed to demonstrate that blacks were systematically excluded from participating in the state party's selection of convention delegates. Mississippi Democrats chose their delegates through a complicated process that began at the precinct level, where they selected representatives to a county convention, which in turn elected delegates to district meetings. This select group traveled to Jackson for the state convention, where they chose the thirty-four delegates and an equal number of alternates to attend the national party conclave in Atlantic City. Blacks attempting to participate in the precinct meetings were turned away at the door in all but a few locations. The district and state conventions, then, were all white, as was the official delegation. At their statewide meeting, the white delegates passed a series of resolutions denouncing the Civil Rights Act of 1964, demanding a purge of the U.S. Supreme Court, and calling for "separation of the races in all phases of our society." Almost all the Democratic Party delegates supported the Republican presidential nominee, Barry Goldwater.

Having been rebuffed by the "white" party, the Freedom Democrats held their own precinct and county meetings, where inexperienced maids and sharecroppers quickly mastered the art of political discourse. "People straight out of tarpaper shacks," one observer reported, "many illiterate, some wearing a (borrowed) suit for the first time . . . without a living memory of political power, yet caught on with some extraordinary inner sense to how the process worked, down to its smallest nuance." Momentum continued to build at the district meetings, which chose representatives to attend the party's state convention in Jackson on August 6.

On the evening of August 4, Pete Seeger was giving a concert at a black church in Meridian. In the middle of a song, someone went to him and whispered in his ear. Seeger stopped singing and spoke to the audience of about two hundred local people: "The bodies of Schwerner, Goodman and Chaney have just been discovered. They were buried deep in the earth." The folksinger later recalled, "There wasn't any shouting. There's just silence. I saw people's lips moving as though in prayer."

A paid informant had revealed that the bodies of the three activists, missing for two months, were buried under an earthen dam in Neshoba County. Later, Ku Klux Klan informants revealed that on the evening of June 21, after the three workers were released from jail, they were stopped and arrested ten miles south of town by Deputy Sheriff Cecil Price, who turned the young men over to a mob of Klansmen. The official autopsy showed that all three had been shot, Schwerner and Goodman once, black activist James Chaney three times. The autopsy also stated that there was no evidence of mutilation or bodily injury. The bodies of the white workers, Schwerner and Goodman, were returned to New York, where they were buried. Questions remained, however, and the Medical Committee for Human Rights sent a leading pathologist, Dr. David Spain, to Jackson to examine James Chaney's body. Spain found that Chaney's lower jaw had been shattered, and the bones in his right shoulder crushed. Spain's conclusion was quoted in newspapers around the world: "I could barely believe the destruction to these frail young bones. In my twenty-five years as a pathologist and medical examiner, I have never seen bones so severely shattered, except in tremendously high speed accidents or airplane crashes. It was obvious to any first-year medical student that this boy had been beaten to a pulp."

What had happened to James Chaney? The FBI's explanation, that his battered body was either the result of contact with the bulldozer that buried the three men in the dam or the dragline used by the FBI to exhume them, was later discredited. Four decades later, Jerry Mitchell, an investigative reporter for the Jackson, Mississippi, *Clarion-Ledger*, uncovered new information about what transpired in Neshoba County that night. Mitchell found a secret report made in early 1965 by an investigator for the Mississippi State Sovereignty Commission that offers a plausible explanation: Chaney broke away from the men who were holding him captive and was shot three times, each shot from a different firearm. The autopsy report, which stated that he was shot once in the back, indicates he was trying to escape. One of the Klan informants had testified that Chaney was killed about forty feet from where Schwerner and Goodman had been shot. Due to the psychology of a lynch mob, a victim attempting to escape was likely to suffer unspeakable brutality once apprehended. Although the controversy continues, Mitchell's conclusion that the Klansmen "just didn't kill the black activist, they tortured him before he died," appears to be the sad truth. (See Document 28.) Late in 1967, an all-white Mississippi jury convicted seven men, including Neshoba County deputy sheriff Cecil Price and Klan leader Sam Bowers, of the federal crime of "violating the rights" of the three activists. The defendants all served short terms and were released from prison by the mid-1970s.

For the delegates assembled at the state convention of the Mississippi Freedom Democratic Party on August 6, the discovery of the three bodies came as a shock but not a surprise. They had long since concluded that the young men had been murdered. Now the task at hand was to select a delegation that would challenge the regular state party at the national convention, and they did so with renewed fervor. (See Document 29.) Twenty-five hundred African Americans and a handful of whites packed the auditorium of the Masonic Temple in Jackson. Each county delegation entered the hall under its own banner, and the group representing Neshoba County received a standing ovation. Several northern state delegations had already pledged to support the MFDP challenge, and Washington attorney Joseph Rauh, who had strong connections to the Democratic Party's liberal wing, had signed on as legal counsel and had agreed to guide the MFDP through the bureaucratic maze of convention regulations.

Rauh explained the process to the delegates assembled in Jackson: In Atlantic City, the MFDP would first take its case to the credentials committee, arguing that blacks had been excluded from the regular party and that unlike the regulars, the MFDP was pledged to support the national party ticket in November. Should the committee refuse to seat the Freedom Democrats, all it took to bring the issue to the convention as a whole—where the issue could be aired before a national television audience—would be for eleven members of the 108-person credentials committee to support the MFDP position, and then later on the convention floor for eight states to demand a roll call. Should the challenge be decided by the convention as a whole, Rauh assured his audience, the chances for success were very good. "Eleven and eight" became the rallying cry for the Freedom Democrats and their supporters.

Ella Baker, the veteran movement organizer now coordinating the effort to win northern support for the challenge, delivered the keynote address. (See Document 30.) After stating that the new party was open to all, "even the son of the planter on whose plantation you work," Baker warned that "until the killing of a black mother's son becomes as important as the killing of a white mother's son, we who believe in freedom cannot rest." She also advised local people not to select convention delegates "who, for the first time, feel their sense of importance and will represent themselves before they represent you." Here she was referring to more conservative, middle-class blacks who had not been part of the movement, but now, because of their status in the community, believed they deserved to be part of the delegation. Although middle-class blacks made up a large portion of the group, the delegation as a whole was militant, including local leaders like Fannie Lou Hamer and Victoria Gray. (See Document 31.) Once selected, the delegation elected SNCC veteran and Tougaloo College graduate Lawrence Guyot as MFDP party chair and SNCC veteran and Rust College graduate Leslie McLemore as vice chair. Aaron Henry was elected chair of the MFDP delegation to Atlantic City, and Fannie Lou Hamer was elected vice chair.

On the evening following the MFDP convention, James Chaney was laid to rest in a black cemetery on a sandy hill four miles south of Meridian. The memorial services were held at the First Union Baptist Church. Mrs. Chaney sat in the first row, her twelve-year-old son, Ben, at her side. For the most part, the service was low-key, with ministers careful not to inflame the emotions of the congregation, in keeping with the wishes of the family and local leaders. Then Dave Dennis, who had headed up the CORE project in Mississippi since the summer of 1962, got up to speak. Looking out at the crowd of people who had lived their lives under the shadow of Jim Crow, Dennis shouted, "I'm sick and tired of going to the funerals of black men who have been murdered by white men. I've got vengeance in my heart and I ask you to be angry with me. . . . If you go back home and take what these white men in Mississippi are doing to us . . . then God damn your souls." (See Document 32.)

THE ATLANTIC CITY CHALLENGE

The Democratic National Convention was to be a coronation of sorts for President Lyndon B. Johnson. No other names would be placed in nomination, and there would be no major platform fights. LBJ was riding high in the polls, and the only item of suspense was his choice of a running mate. But the sixty-four blacks and four whites who made up the delegation of the Freedom Democratic Party threw a monkey wrench into the president's plans for an orchestrated convention. For four days, the Mississippi Freedom Democrats' challenge was the major story in Atlantic City.

The MFDP delegates arrived in the resort town by bus on Friday, August 21, the day before the credentials committee hearing. Housed in the small, run-down Gem Hotel, about a mile from the convention center, the delegates quickly set about their appointed task, fanning out over the boardwalk, buttonholing delegates, and bringing them the word on the righteousness of their challenge. While it might appear that their case was irrefutable—after all, the regular white delegation was not only segregationist, it was not even going to support the national ticket—there was one problem. Lyndon Johnson strongly opposed the Freedom Democrats and their challenge. (See Document 33.)

Johnson knew that his opponent in November would be the nation's leading conservative, Senator Barry Goldwater. Their differences on the issue of race could not have been clearer: LBJ had pushed the Civil Rights Act through Congress; Goldwater voted against it. Johnson took pride in his civil rights record. He opposed the challenge on political grounds, fearing that if the delegation were seated, the other southern states would walk out of the convention, and Goldwater would win the election. In the weeks preceding the convention, Johnson was in constant contact with his aides. (See Document 34.) He confided to Senator Hubert Humphrey, "There's no justification in messing with the Freedom Party at all. If we mess with the group of Negroes that were elected to nothing, and throw out the governor and elected officials of the state . . . we will lose 15 states without even campaigning." Johnson became obsessed with the challenge, employing thirty undercover FBI agents at the convention, who wiretapped Martin Luther King's hotel telephone and installed microphone surveillance at SNCC's headquarters. (See Document 35.)

Unaware that the president of the United States was employing tactics against them normally reserved for gangsters or spies, the MFDP went about its business and made its presence known. Supporters set up a round-the-clock vigil on the boardwalk outside the convention hall. There they displayed giant pictures of the martyred civil rights workers and a replica of the burnt-out shell of Mickey Schwerner's station wagon. Freedom songs filled the air, and members of the delegation came by to make speeches. Stokely Carmichael recalled, "Every delegate going into the arena had to pass our vigil. It was all unusually powerful and moving, and many a delegate stopped, looked, listened, and volunteered his vote before going in." When the credentials committee convened on Saturday, TV network cameras were there to cover the proceedings live. First up was E. K. Collins, representing the all-white Mississippi delegation, who vehemently denied that blacks had difficulty voting in Mississippi. MFDP speakers argued that the convention should seat their delegation because blacks had been shut out of the Mississippi Democratic Party. The Freedom Democrats had observed all regulations in selecting their delegation and had pledged their loyalty to the national ticket. Joe Rauh brought forth a number of witnesses, including delegation chair Aaron Henry, national committeeman Ed King, and Martin Luther King, who told committee members that they "must recognize the Freedom party delegation." Yet that day even Dr. King was overshadowed by former sharecropper Fannie Lou Hamer.

The several million Americans watching the hearings on television knew little about Mrs. Hamer, but as she described life on the plantation, her eviction when she attempted to register to vote, and, most dramatically, her beating in the Winona jail, it became apparent that hers was an authentic voice describing the daily horror of life in the closed society. This was high drama, and it did not go unnoticed in the White House, where Lyndon Johnson called a press conference in the middle of her testimony. The networks dutifully cut away, thinking Johnson might announce his choice for vice president. Instead, the president made no such announcement, nor did he talk about anything newsworthy. By the time he finished speaking, so had Fannie Lou Hamer, but the networks played back her testimony that night, where a prime-time audience heard Mrs. Hamer conclude, in a voice filled with emotion, "If the Freedom Party is not seated now I question America." (See Document 36.)

Immediately after Mrs. Hamer finished speaking, telegrams of support for the Freedom Democrats began pouring in. When the credentials committee reconvened on Sunday afternoon, Joe Rauh was confident. He had seventeen committee members pledged to sign a minority report supporting the MFDP, six more than he needed, and ten states, including New York, Michigan, and California, to ensure that there would be a roll call on the convention floor. This surge of support sent President Johnson into a tailspin. He told aides that he was going to refuse nomination for another term, because "I do not believe I can physically and mentally carry the responsibilities of . . . the world and the nigras and the South and so forth." Of course the president changed his mind—and then went into attack mode.

First, credentials committee chair Governor David Lawrence of Pennsylvania formed a subcommittee to resolve the Mississippi question, appointing as its chair Minnesota attorney general Walter Mondale, a protégé of Senator Hubert Humphrey. It was now an open secret that Humphrey's chances for gaining the vice presidential nomination depended on his finding a solution to the MFDP challenge that was acceptable to the White House. The president's operatives on the floor began contacting the members of the credentials committee who were supporting the challengers, promising political rewards—or punishment—depending on how they voted on Mississippi. The hearings dragged on for two more days, with no decision on the challenge. With the passage of time, the MFDP's support on the credentials committee began to erode. Years later, Walter Mondale conceded, "Frankly, part of what we were doing in our subcommittee was buying time to keep the dispute off the convention floor."

Everything came to a head on Tuesday afternoon at the final credentials committee meeting. There Mondale came forward with a three-part proposal approved by President Johnson. First, MFDP representatives Aaron Henry and Ed King would be seated as at-large delegates, with the rest of the delegation "welcomed as honored guests of this convention." Second, only those members of the Mississippi regulars who signed a loyalty oath agreeing to support the party's nominees in November would be seated. Finally—and in the long run most important—the national Democratic Party pledged to eliminate racial discrimination in all future conventions. While the credentials committee considered the Mondale motion, Humphrey convened a meeting with MFDP supporters, including Martin Luther King, Aaron Henry, Ed King, and Bob Moses. His purpose was to sell the compromise to them. Moses did not favor the proposal, but he, Henry, and Ed King all agreed that the MFDP delegation would have to decide the question. At that point, one of Humphrey's aides burst in to say that there was important news on television. Everyone rushed into the next room to hear a bulletin that the credentials committee had just approved a two-seat "compromise" and that this was a great victory for the civil rights forces. Believing he had been sandbagged, Moses stormed out of the room and grabbed a cab back to meet with the delegates to assure them that neither he nor anyone else associated with the challenge had accepted the proposed deal.

The combination of political pressure from the White House and the compromise itself all but dissolved the MFDP's support on the credentials committee. There would be no minority report brought to the convention, no roll call vote. The Freedom Democrats met late Tuesday afternoon and rejected the compromise, which had been pushed through without their knowledge or input, but their response had no bearing on the final outcome. That night, the convention approved the compromise by voice vote with no discussion. Angry supporters staged a protest outside the convention hall, and later in the evening twenty-one members of the Freedom Party delegation, having received credentials from friendly delegates from other states, moved onto the convention floor and occupied the seats of the regulars, all but four of whom had refused to sign the loyalty oath and left the convention.

The sight of black Mississippians engaging in acts of civil disobedience made liberal Democrats uncomfortable, and they made one final effort to persuade the Freedom Party to accept the compromise and end their protests. Aaron Henry, who was now openly supporting the compromise, called for a caucus on Wednesday morning, where the delegation heard from the leaders of the civil rights establishment. Bayard Rustin, the chief architect of the March on Washington, told the delegates it was time for them to face political reality: "You must accept the compromise." Martin Luther King did not employ his considerable oratorical skills to sway the delegation, but he said that Humphrey promised him that "there would be a new day in Mississippi if you accept this proposal."

Opponents pointed out that the compromise recognized the legitimacy of the all-white delegation; that if Aaron Henry and Ed King took their seats, they would be registered as at-large delegates and would not represent Mississippi; and that the Johnson forces did not have the right to decide who the MFDP delegates would be. The promise that things would be different in 1968 seemed empty, since only a handful of blacks could vote in Mississippi. Aside from these particulars, the grassroots contingent was furious that the proposal had been sprung on them after the fact and that the people whom they had trusted appeared to have sold them out. (See Document 37.)

At the conclusion of the speeches, everyone except the delegates left the room. As the debate began, the issue was in doubt. A number of the delegates who had rejected the compromise the day before were now having second thoughts, prepared to resign themselves to the inevitable, to declare victory and go home. In the end, though, it was Fannie Lou Hamer, now the national symbol of grassroots activism, who stated the case simply but powerfully. "We didn't come all the way up here to compromise for no more than we'd gotten here," she said. "We didn't come all this way for no two seats, 'cause all of us is tired." After hours of discussion and debate, the Freedom Democrats once again rejected the Atlantic City compromise. (See Document 38.)

"For many people," observed SNCC's Joyce Ladner, "Atlantic City was the end of innocence." For the radical young activists who had been working in Mississippi for years, the Democratic Convention marked a turning point. SNCC veteran Cleveland Sellers later described his disillusionment with the political establishment: "Never again were we lulled into believing that our task was exposing injustices so that the 'good' people of America could eliminate them. . . . After Atlantic City, the struggle was not for civil rights, but for liberation." Sellers, Stokely Carmichael, and a number of other organizers alienated by the failure of the MFDP challenge would become the vanguard of the Black Power movement of the late 1960s and 1970s.

But many of the native Mississippians who made up the rank and file of the Freedom Democratic Party came away from Atlantic City with a feeling of accomplishment. Among them was delegate Unita Blackwell, who was later elected mayor of her Mississippi town. "Even though we didn't win our challenge, the experience didn't feel like defeat to me," she wrote in her autobiography. "We had, in fact, knocked out most of the regulars from being seated, and we had drawn national attention to our new party and to problems within the national Democratic organization. We had stood proud and strong." (See Document 39.)

Returning from Atlantic City, the Mississippi Freedom Democratic Party, led by Lawrence Guyot, endorsed the Johnson-Humphrey ticket and held another "freedom vote," running its own slate of candidates for national office. In 1965, the MFDP challenged the seating of the Mississippi delegation to the House of Representatives, claiming that because blacks had been excluded from the polls, the election of the white segregationists was unconstitutional. Although it lost the challenge, the party had focused national attention on the problems facing black southerners attempting to register and vote. Along with the more publicized SCLC campaign in Selma, Alabama, the congressional challenge of the Freedom Democrats ensured passage of the Voting Rights Act of 1965, a law that changed the political course of the South—and the nation.

CONCLUSION

When in the spring of 1964 COFO activists started to plan for a summer project, they had no idea of the consequences of their actions, that Freedom Summer would become, in the words of Stokely Carmichael, "the boldest, most dramatic, and traumatic single event of the entire movement." After that summer, the state of Mississippi would never be the same. The summer project, grudging compliance with the new civil rights act, and the peaceful desegregation of a handful of elementary schools in the fall of 1964 marked the end of "massive resistance." White Mississippians no longer spoke with a single voice. Segregation remained a fact of life throughout much of the state, but the Jim Crow signs began to come down, and by the late 1960s it was no longer unusual to see blacks eating in white-owned restaurants, staying in local motels, or patronizing the previously segregated public libraries. A degree of civility had come to the Magnolia State. The movement had made it possible for the black middle class to make significant gains. By the early 1970s, Mississippi corporations and local governments were employing blacks in positions previously reserved for whites. The major victory of the movement, however, was the substantial reduction in the use of terror to control the state's black population. Blacks had won the right to organize their communities and to take political action without fear of brutal reprisal. Racial violence remained a fact of life, but the systematic use of terror, condoned and often directed by law enforcement officers, gradually abated.

Nowhere was racial progress more evident than in the political arena. The Freedom Democratic Party remained active and, in 1967, schoolteacher Robert Clark became the first African American to serve in the Mississippi legislature in the twentieth century. The MFDP was, however, being challenged by a coalition of middle-class blacks led by Aaron Henry, who had become alienated from COFO after Atlantic City, and white moderates from the Delta such as Hodding Carter III. In a display of unity, the competing factions joined together to form the "loyalist" coalition, and in 1968 that group was officially recognized at the Democratic National Convention in Chicago, replacing the white "regular" faction. Thanks to the Voting Rights Act, now hundreds of thousands of blacks had registered and were voting, and by the 1980s, Mississippi led the nation in the number of black elected officials. Black Mississippians had come a long way since Atlantic City.

It was not until the twenty-first century, however, that Americans felt the full impact of the Atlantic City challenge. The Democratic Party's nomination of Barack Obama in 2008 as its presidential standard-bearer was a historic event that had its origins in the party's pledge in 1964 to abolish racial discrimination in all state delegations. That action was, in the words of Walter Mondale, "the civil rights act for the Democratic Party." In an interview on Inauguration Day 2009, Bob Moses observed that "the crucial thing [about Obama's election] . . . was the 1964 challenge of the Mississippi Freedom Democratic Party to the National Democratic Convention. . . . That action, more than anything else, opened up the national party structure." Distinguished civil rights activist Roger Wilkins put it bluntly: Obama would not be president "but for the Mississippi freedom movement."

Despite all these achievements, both locally and nationally, Freedom Summer and the Mississippi movement failed to bring about the social revolution envisioned by the militant activists. Whites continue to hold most of the positions of political power and to dominate all aspects of economic life. In the second decade of the twenty-first century, Mississippi still led the nation in poverty, infant mortality, and illiteracy. Yet if black Mississippians did not achieve all their goals during the movement years, in the decades following World War II they did bring about extraordinary changes in a state that had been locked up in the caste system for nearly a century. They had transformed the closed society, opened up the political process to African Americans, and made it possible for new generations to build on the solid foundation laid by that band of brothers and sisters during the civil rights years. Bob Moses once observed that the movement had "brought Mississippi, for better or worse, up to the level of the rest of the country." That was no small achievement. It also reminds us of the distance still to be traveled.

PART TWO

The Documents

1

The Long Black Freedom Struggle

1

CONGRESS OF RACIAL EQUALITY

Poster Announcing a Mass Meeting Where Mrs. Fannie Chaney Will Speak

August 27, 1964

This poster publicizes a mass meeting where the mother of slain civil rights worker James Chaney spoke on the work of Freedom Summer. Mrs. Fannie Chaney worked to bring justice to Meridian, Mississippi, before her son James joined CORE, and she continued as a movement activist after Freedom Summer ended. Her activism was an important influence on James. The courage she demonstrated by speaking in public barely two months after the killing shows the importance of overcoming fear and challenging segregation directly. What do you imagine was the mood in the room that night as she spoke? How do you imagine white Mississippians felt about this gathering? What does the poster suggest about Mississippi movement activists and about Freedom Summer?

HEAR!   HEAR!
HOW OUR BROTHERS
Died For Freedom
AND HOW WE ARE CARRYING
ON THE FIGHT IN MISSISSIPPI

Mickey Schwerner   James Chaney   Andrew Goodman

HEAR
Mrs. Fanny Chaney
Courageous Mother of James Chaney
At New Zion Baptist Church
2319 THIRD STREET
THURS., AUG. 27, 1964
7:30 P. M.
CORE

Danny Lyon/Magnum Photos.

2

NAACP

M Is for Mississippi and Murder

1955

In response to the Brown v. Board of Education *decision, whites stepped up their resistance to civil rights activity, with tactics ranging from economic sanctions to acts of violence. There were several racial murders in 1955, none of which resulted in convictions. That November, the NAACP put out a pamphlet on the spate of killings and sent it to decision makers in and outside the South. Two of the victims were civil rights leaders engaged in voter registration. The third, Emmett Till, a fourteen-year-old from Chicago, allegedly flirted with a white woman in a store. This pamphlet makes clear the stakes faced by anyone who challenged white supremacy in the Magnolia State.*

Backdrop for Murder

A Few Killings—An Associated Press dispatch written by Sam Johnson and datelined from Jackson, Miss., September 9, 1954, says in part:

"White men who want to keep segregation in force are banding into 'citizens councils' throughout Mississippi, several legislators said today.

"The peaceful approach was emphasized by several leaders in Washington County . . . But some other legislators from the Delta and other 'black counties' where Negroes outnumber whites, predicted bloodshed . . .

"One said 'a few killings' would be the best thing for the state just before the people vote on a proposed constitutional amendment empowering the Legislature to abolish public schools.

"The 'few killings' would make certain that the people would approve the amendment and 'would save a lot of bloodshed later on,' he added." . . .

In this climate of opinion which derides the courts and the rule of law, which harps on violence, sometimes nakedly and sometimes through the device of repeated disavowal, three persons were murdered in Mississippi between May 7 and August 28, 1955.

National Association for the Advancement of Colored People Papers, Manuscript Division, Library of Congress, Washington, D.C., group III, box A-230.

GETTING AWAY WITH MURDER

Near midnight on May 7 the Rev. George W. Lee was driving home in his town of Belzoni, Miss., in Humphreys County. Another car overtook him on a dark street. There were two shotgun blasts from the passing car and Rev. Lee slumped over his steering wheel with his jaw shot away. He died before he could be taken to a hospital.

Rev. Lee was the first of his race to register to vote in Humphreys County and he had urged others to register. He had told a friend on the afternoon of his death day that he had been ordered to remove his name from the registration list. He had refused to do so.

No arrests have been made.

The Sheriff said the lead pellets in Rev. Lee's jaw and neck "could have been fillings from his teeth."

In the broad daylight of Saturday afternoon, August 13, Lamar Smith was shot dead in front of the courthouse at Brookhaven, Miss. He had been active in getting voters out for the primary election August 2 and was working on the run-off primary scheduled for August 23.

Brookhaven is the home town of Circuit Judge Tom Brady who has been active in the formation of White Citizens Councils. . . .

A grand jury on September 21, 1955, failed to return an indictment against the three men arrested in connection with the Smith murder. . . .

Sometime after 2 a.m. on August 28, Emmett Louis Till, 14, who had come to the town of Money, Miss., from Chicago to visit his great-uncle, Moses Wright, was kidnapped at gun point, beaten, shot and thrown into the Tallahatchie River.

Two half-brothers, J. W. Milam, 36, and Roy Bryant, 24, were tried for murder in Sumner, Miss., in Tallahatchie County where the body was found. The two admitted taking the Till boy from his uncle's cabin because he allegedly "wolf-whistled" at Mrs. Bryant three or four days earlier, but said they released him unharmed a short time later. Moses Wright identified Milam from the witness stand as the man who had come to his home with a drawn gun, demanded the Till boy, took him from his bed and pushed him into a waiting car.

An all-white jury (only voters may serve on juries and none of the county's 19,000 Negroes is permitted to vote) took only one hour and seven minutes to acquit the two defendants. . . .

The Sheriff said the body was not that of the Till boy, but was part of a plot by the National Association for the Advancement of Colored People.

John C. Whitten, one of the five attorneys defending Milam and Bryant, in addressing the jury said: "I am sure every last Anglo-Saxon one of you has the courage to free these men . . ."

THIS IS MISSISSIPPI

These were not murders of passion, or for profit, but futile, cold, brutal murders to bolster a theory of superiority based upon skin color.

3

STATE OF MISSISSIPPI

Voter Registration Form

1950s

This document is the voter registration form used by the state of Mississippi from the 1950s up until passage of the federal Voting Rights Act of 1965. Note especially questions 18, 19, and 20. Are these "trick" questions? (The county registrar alone decided whether the applicant had passed this test.)

Sworn Written Application for Registration

(By reason of the provisions of Sections 241, 241-A and 244 of the Constitution of Mississippi and relevant statutes of the State of Mississippi, the applicant for registration, if not physically disabled is required to fill in this form in his own handwriting in the presence of the registrar and without assistance or suggestion of any person or memorandum.)

1. Write the date of this application _____
2. What is your full name? _____
3. State your age and date of birth _____
4. What is your occupation? _____
5. Where is your business carried on? (Give city, town or village, and street address, if any, but if none, post office address.) If not engaged in business, so state _____

Papers of R. Edwin King Jr., L. Zenobia Coleman Library, Tougaloo College, Tougaloo, Miss.

6. By whom are you employed? (Give name and street address, if any, but if none, post office address.) If not employed, so state _____

7. Where is your place of residence in the county and district where you propose to register? (Give city, town or village, and street address, if any, but if none, post office address.) _____

8. Are you a citizen of the United States and an inhabitant of Mississippi? _____

9. How long have you resided in Mississippi? _____

10. How long have you resided in the election district or precinct in which you propose to register? _____

11. State your last previous places of residence. (Give street address, if any, but if none, post office address.) _____

12. Are you a minister of the gospel in charge of an organized church, or the wife of such a minister? If so what church? (Give address in each instance.) _____

13. Check which oath you desire to take: (1) General _____
(2) Minister's _____ (3) Minister's wife: _____ (4) If under 21 years at present, but will be 21 years old by date of general election. _____

14. If there is more than one person of your same name in the precinct, by what name do you wish to be called? _____

15. Have you ever been convicted of any of the following crimes: bribery, theft, arson, obtaining money or goods under false pretenses, perjury, forgery, embezzlement, or bigamy? _____

16. Have you ever been convicted of any other crime (excepting misdemeanors for traffic violations)? _____

17. If your answer to question 15 or 16 is "Yes," name the crime or crimes of which you have been convicted, and the year, court, and place of such conviction or convictions: _____
_____
_____

18. Write and copy in the space below, Section _____ of the Constitution of Mississippi: (Instructions to Registrar: You will designate the Section of the Constitution and point out same to applicant) _____

_____

_____

19. Write in the space below a reasonable interpretation (the meaning) of the Section of the Constitution of Mississippi which you have just copied: _____

_____

_____

20. Write in the space below a statement setting forth your understanding of the duties and obligations of citizenship under a constitutional form of government. _____

_____

_____

4

TOM GAITHER AND BOB MOSES

Report on Voter Registration—Projected Program
January 27, 1962

The Council of Federated Organizations was originally an ad hoc group led by Aaron Henry that met once with Governor Ross Barnett during the freedom rides. In February 1962, SNCC's Bob Moses, Tom Gaither of CORE, and Aaron Henry and Medgar Evers of the NAACP met to revamp COFO into an organization incorporating all national, state, and local protest groups operating in the state. In no other state did the leading civil rights organizations operate under the same umbrella agency. CORE's Dave Dennis observed that "the Negro people of Mississippi needed some organization which could belong to them (as opposed

Congress of Racial Equality Papers, 1959–1976, microfilm edition (Bethesda, Md.: University Publications of America, 1984), reel 41, frames 212–14. Hereafter cited, CORE Papers.

to their belonging to it), which could serve as a unifying force among the isolated Negro communities." The origins of much of the summer project appear in this document. Indeed, it is hard to imagine Freedom Summer without this coordinated effort of local leaders.

I. We understand that several philanthropic organizations are donating money for a concerted drive to register Negro voters across the deep South. The money, as we understand it, is to be derived primarily among the following Civil Rights organizations: NAACP, SCLC, CORE, SNCC. . . .

> We also understand . . . that most of the organizations are planning to concentrate their efforts in big cities. If this is true, then most of Mississippi will be excluded from the drive. Even if this proves false, we feel there is a necessity for coordinating the activities of the organizations to avoid duplication, confusion and a general lack of direction.
>
> To ensure that Mississippians will receive full benefit from the monies donated by the foundations and administered by the Civil Rights organizations, we propose that the following steps be taken:

1. A state-wide coordinating council will be established, to be composed of individuals representing . . . organizations interested in promoting voter registration. (We receive and work with personnel from the various Civil Rights groups.)

2. That representatives of SNCC, CORE, NAACP, and SCLC, working in Mississippi . . . call . . . an initial meeting as soon as possible in February. . . .

II. We offer the following suggestions for a tentative program:

A. Basic Goals:

> Since the fundamental politics unit in the state is found at the county level, one of the goals of the program should be the development of leadership at this level to ensure an ongoing program in voter registration and in furthering the political aspirations and aims of the Negro.
>
> We know, however, that in many rural counties such an organization is not feasible at this time; in this case a wider

organization, encompassing several adjoining counties, including, if possible, one which contains a large urban population, should be established. . . .

We must aim to unite the various leaders in a given area through personal contact and cooperation on a common program, in an effort to decrease chances of reprisals against those located in tough areas, and increase moral and effective organization.

B. Program in Urban Areas

Again, following the political outline of the state and the concentration of Negroes, it seems natural to spend our heaviest efforts in the second, third, and fourth congressional districts, where the Negroes comprise 50%, 66%, and 45% respectively of the population. . . .

Cities such as Greenville, Clarksdale, Jackson, Vicksburg, and Natchez, where Negroes are allowed to vote without fear of physical violence or economic reprisals, but where apathy, ignorance, and long deprivation have dulled the appetite for the ballot, should be given special consideration and the types of long range program best suited for each city carefully spelled out in conjunction with the leaders of the city. It seems imperative that all groups now working on voter registration within a given city, coordinate their efforts and present a unified program for the people of their jurisdiction. . . .

County seat towns such as Tylertown, Liberty and Fayette should be hit hard and fast and at unannounced intervals, or not at all, as the local population is too easily exposed to pressures and threats of physical violence and therefore too easily frightened away.

C. Proposed Organization for Rural Areas

The chief institution in the rural community in which we may find leadership and support will be the church. We should not however overlook the possibility that we may find that we are forced to work with other organizations, and individuals who are somewhat free of economic pressures.

Preparation for projects should include visits to communities to be worked in an effort to meet community leaders, and to, whenever possible, actually live with people in the community so that a real relationship between all concerned may be realized.

Determine which community organizations will work with you in the project, by personal contacts. Call a meeting to orientate participants in the objectives of the project, being careful to give considerable weight to their observations and considerations in which general approach should be used.

Try to find some place where a local headquarters can be maintained, noting that it may be unwise to remain in the very small communities over a week or more at a time.

Attempt to recruit volunteer workers for a door to door campaign, in an effort to channel the persons contacted to the headquarters for specific detailed instruction in voting and registration procedures. . . .

Schools to teach the basic Three R's should be set up to supplement the lack of efficiency in these areas wherever necessary.

D. Staff

In the foregoing pages we have set forth a structure and a program wherein all of the organizations working can find common ground for a well-coordinated effort in voter registration in Mississippi. To do this job effectively, staff people will be needed at the following levels:

1. To set up the program in detail, arrange for a meeting of the members of the coordinating council, and see that they have a copy of the proposed program in time enough to obtain suggestions and comments of their local organizations.

Bob Moses
Tom Gaither

5

CHARLES McLAURIN

Notes on Organizing

1965

---

*Mississippi was transformed through the hard work of community orga-
nizers. In the following document, Charles McLaurin discusses his work
as a SNCC field secretary. Medgar Evers had recruited the young Jackson
State student into the movement, and in early 1962 McLaurin was working in Sunflower County, the heart of the Delta. There he met Fannie Lou
Hamer and became her trusted confidant. McLaurin wrote two essays to
help prepare others for the challenges that lay ahead. In the first essay,
McLaurin focuses on the hard work of community organizing. Written as
a kind of blueprint for civil rights workers, the lessons contained in this
essay remain valuable for any kind of organizing work. Organizers need
to become part of the communities where they work. Their job is to cul-
tivate local leaders, work with them, and stay out of the limelight. What
were the principal challenges that civil rights organizers faced? What
were the principal goals of civil rights organizing? What are the qualities
needed to become a good organizer?*

A SNCC worker should never take a leadership role in the community
unless he is in his own community. A SNCC worker should give the
responsibility of leadership to the community person or persons whom
he has or is building. The SNCC worker should give form and guidance
to the people's organization, and/or their programs.

I think that in each area one faces different kinds of problems. I've
attempted to state some of the problems found in small communities
such as Ruleville and Indianola, Miss.

The larger, more middle-class communities will be somewhat
different.

I think you at first meet the people on their own terms, or you lose.

Student Nonviolent Coordinating Committee Papers, 1959–1972 (Sanford, N.C.: Micro-
filming Corp. of America, 1981), reel 40, frames 52–55. Hereafter cited, SNCC Papers.

Entering the Community

There are two ways to enter a community: the *invited* and the *uninvited* way. . . .

An *uninvited* worker faces many difficulties; first, he is unexpected and in many cases unwanted by the do-nothing leaders of the community. He is a stranger to the people, and therefore, he is alone in a strange place. If he is to be successful, he must become a part of the community. . . .

Making Contact

Since you have found a place to stay, say with a family, then the work starts, and it starts just as do most things, in the home.

You should spend as much time as the family has talking to them, because they have information about the people — both white and black. They have been there all of their lives; they know the community; they know the people who will help. Take time and talk to them; ask questions, for it is here that you get real *community education.* . . .

Canvass the whole community one afternoon. Talk with the people, laugh with them, joke with them; do most anything that gets some attention on you, or on some kind of conversation. It is very important to learn what bugs them. It may happen that they are thinking about trying to get the vote. You'll know when they talk.

The most important thing is to move the community by action; the community will move when the people move. The people will move when they are *motivated*.

Some Ways of Motivating People

Canvass two or three days, the first week. Do not worry too much about what you hear from the people. If you just talk and ask questions, some of them may talk about Chicago or Welfare checks; this is good, this is what is on their minds presently.

During canvassing, be sure to take down the names and addresses of the people who talked, who seemed to you that there is hope in them. This could be only two people; or it could be ten. No matter what the number is, these are contacts. You have a small group of people. Now you need a *place to meet* with them. Try to get a church or an empty building; if you cannot get either, use one of the people's homes for a meeting place. Again, start with the people where you live; ask to hold the meeting there.

Building Leaders

The reason for using this home is that you have now found that dependable leadership does not exist. You must, from this little group, find and build a leader or leaders. How?

In this meeting, plan some kind of action. You put suggestions before the group. Let them talk over the suggestions, about paved streets, stop signs, street lights, or recreational facilities, and how the vote can get these and more.

You may need to hold ten or more of these kinds of meetings; at the same time, trying to get a church, getting the word out about the house meeting by leafletting or word of mouth. But let it get out! Elect a chairman to chair the meetings; you should not do this after the first meeting. Each meeting, give more and more of the responsibilities to this group, and as the group grows, form committees so as to involve more of the people.

To overcome the fear, many of the things above mentioned will apply. By getting the people together, they will see that they are not alone. . . . The feeling of being close together will help overcome the fear.

Apathy will disappear when you give the people some responsibility. . . . At first the family educated you; now together they are educating each other.

6

CHARLES McLAURIN

To Overcome Fear
1965

Charles McLaurin's candid essay on overcoming fear recalls how he was inspired by the courage of three local women who went to the courthouse to register to vote. Among the many challenges of organizing in the black community during the civil rights movement was the real threat of violence from white racists. In this essay, McLaurin admits to being afraid and suggests that organizers and local people are never without fear; rather they learn to overcome their fear in order to act in the face of terror. What are the sources of fear that McLaurin notes? How does living in fear impact human personality? How did Charles McLaurin learn to overcome his fear and gain the courage to act? What are the differences between fearlessness and overcoming fear?

The first people that I accompanied to the Sunflower County Courthouse in Indianola, Miss. gave me the spirit and courage to continue.

I will always remember August 22, 1962 as the day that I became a man . . . on this day I was to test myself for courage and the ability to move in the face of fear and danger. . . .

. . . That morning, I had been around to the homes of people who had given me their names as persons willing to . . . attempt to register to vote. I was very disappointed, I had only been able to find three of the ten. The others because of fear had left home rather than say so to me.

Since I was going down to the Courthouse for my first time I too was afraid; not of dying and not of the man (Mr. Charlie) per se, but the powers of the sheriff's department, the police department, the courts; these are the powers and forces which keep Negroes in their so-called places. . . .

I had only three people to go to the courthouse. This was the day I learned that the numbers were not important. I learned that a faithful few were better than an uncertain ten.

SNCC Papers, reel 40, frames 52–55.

These three old ladies, whose ages ranged from 65 to 85, knew the white man and his ways . . . and on this day, they would come face to face with his sons and daughters to say, "We Must be Free; Now!"

Tommie Johnson, son of one of the ladies active in the movement in Ruleville, was to carry us . . . on 49 highway.

We drove past an American service station operated by three white brothers known as the Woolenhams. These were bad brothers. They were known to beat up Negroes getting off the Greyhound bus when it put them off there. They also pulled guns on Negroes who asked for air in their car tires. As we passed this station I could not help but watch to see if they noticed the car, for this car had taken six brave ladies down weeks earlier, and all the white people knew it. On and on passing the people in the cotton fields; trucks and busses along the sides of the highway; men, women, and children moving to the rhythm of the beat of the hoe; working, hoping, and forever saying "lord my time ain't long, this work will soon be over, I'll be free." . . .

Doddsville, five miles south of Ruleville . . . is the home of U.S. Senator . . . James O. Eastland. . . .

Doddsville where many years ago the burning of Negroes was a Sunday spectacle where whites young and old delighted at this evil which killed the spirit of the old Negroes and set the stage for the place-fixing of young ones not yet born.

On and on my eyes taking in as much at a glance as possible. The old ladies talking, telling the stories of the years gone by; me with knees shaking, mouth closed tightly so as to not let them hear the fear in my voice. . . .

I was going to face the man (Mr. Charlie) in the Courthouse. I was filled with fear but this I must do; do this or continue to *die*. Not that I was dead and walking as such, but one who is alive in real life but dead in mind, dead in ability to say, do, or to act in a way that would give attention to ones present in society.

We turned off the highway and again we drove south, this time through a neighborhood, a white neighborhood. Then around a corner and there was the courthouse, the police station, and the sheriff's department. All of the big powers together. . . .

As I opened the door to get out I got a feeling in my stomach that made me feel weak. Sweat started to form on my forehead. . . . At this point I was no longer in command, the three old ladies were leading me, I was following them. They got out of the car and went up the walk to the courthouse as if this was the long walk that led to the Golden Gate of Heaven, their hands held high. I watched from a short distance behind them; the pride with which they walked. The strong convictions that they held. . . . I stepped outside the door and waited, thinking how it was that these ladies who have been victimized by white faces all of their lives would suddenly walk up to the man and say, *I want to vote.* This did something to me. It told me something. It was like a voice speaking to me, as I stood there alone, in a strange place and an unknown land. This voice told me that although these old ladies knew the risk involved in their being here they were still willing to try. It said you are the light, let it shine and people will know you, and they will follow you, if you show the way they will go, with or without you.

So they did. . . . I told them what to do and when that day came I followed them. The people are the true leaders. We need only to move them; to show them. Then watch and learn.

7

NICHOLAS deB. KATZENBACH

Memorandum for the President on the Use of Marshals, Troops, and Other Federal Law Enforcement in Mississippi

July 1, 1964

In this memorandum to President Lyndon Johnson, Deputy Attorney General Nicholas deB. Katzenbach outlines the government's position on federal intervention in the affairs of individual states. This doctrine, which became known as "Federalism," had as its basic premise that "the responsibility for the preservation of law and order . . . is the responsibility of the local authorities." Only when local officials totally lost control of a situation would the federal government respond with outside force. A group of law professors had challenged this interpretation of the Constitution. Katzenbach's brief, in response, offers an extended rationale in support of the government's position. Does his argument make sense to you?

Memo, Katzenbach to the President, July 1, 1964, attached to memo, Katzenbach to Lee White, July 1, 1964, "Ex HU 2/ST 24 1/1/64–7/15/64," White House Central Files (WHCF), box 26, LBJ Library.

There are considerable pressures from civil rights groups and from some Members of Congress to station federal personnel in Mississippi as a method of preventing further acts of violence against civil rights workers there. These proposals range from those which urge, in effect, the occupation of Mississippi by federal troops to those which suggest that a modest number of United States marshals or FBI agents be strategically placed to help protect civil rights workers.

All of these proposals raise mixed problems of law, policy, and practicality. The purpose of this memorandum is to clarify those problems.

I—The Legal Background

In general, federal law enforcement efforts have traditionally been designed to supplement and support the efforts of state law enforcement personnel rather than to replace them. Under the Constitution, the States have exclusive jurisdiction over most aspects of law enforcement. . . . It is State and local law which defines and punishes crimes such as murder, assault, rioting, disturbing the peace, vandalism, and so on, which seldom also involve violations of federal law. . . .

If marshals or agents of the Bureau are used in any obvious way as guards in Mississippi, without the active support and cooperation of local officials, local law enforcement will tend to break down. This is not merely because local officials resent the intervention of outsiders, although that is an obvious factor. The fact is that in Mississippi the use of federal law enforcement personnel, particularly marshals, is regarded by the public as provocative and might well give rise to more breaches of the peace than would otherwise occur. Particularly if the civil rights workers involved engage in demonstrations and other mass activities while accompanied by marshals, their function will soon cease to be one of preventing clandestine violence and become one of maintaining public order among considerable numbers of people over a large area. In that situation, our experience is that without the support of local officials the maintenance of order requires the use of troops. . . .

III—Use of Troops

The federal statutes relevant to the use of military force in connection with civil disturbances are 10 U.S.C. 331–334. Section 331 authorizes the President to supply armed forces at the call of a State legislature or governor to suppress an insurrection. Sections 332 and 333 authorize the President to use the armed forces without a request by State or local authorities in order to enforce federal law. Section 334 provides that whenever the President considers it necessary to use the armed forces pursuant to the three preceding sections of the Code, "he shall, by proclamation, immediately order the insurgents to disperse and retire peaceably to their abodes within a limited time.". . .

"Unless there is some special reason which seems to make imperative the immediate use of the troops, or until all efforts to effect a peaceful settlement have failed and violence threatens of a nature beyond the ability of the local and state governments to control, the president is wise to avoid recourse to force. To use the troops only when no other solution seems possible has been the most frequent presidential practice—a practice the value of which is attested by the fact that it has met with complete success.". . .

There are, of course, immense practical problems involved in the use of troops, of which possibly the worst one is that it becomes difficult to find a way to withdraw. Local authorities tend to abdicate all law enforcement responsibility, leaving the troops without adequate legal tools—short of a declaration of martial law—to perform routine law enforcement functions for which they have little training.

IV—Conclusion

The group of professors which has publicly taken issue with the statement attributed (inaccurately) to the Attorney General that there was no adequate legal basis for federal law enforcement in Mississippi is hard to dispute. They assume the complete breakdown of State law enforcement as a result of Klan activity and Klan connections with local sheriffs and deputies. On that factual assumption the President could, as a legal matter, invoke the authority of sections 332 and 333. There is, of course, considerable information available that could be used to support that assumption as to some areas in Mississippi. But in view of the extreme seriousness of the use of those sections, I believe that the government should have more evidence than it presently has of the inability of State and local officials to maintain law and order—as a matter of wisdom as well as of law. Furthermore, vigorous investigation and prosecution where federal crimes are involved may serve, in conjunction with State police action, to forestall the serious breakdown which those sections of the statute contemplate.

As indicated above, the problems of using large numbers of federal civilian law enforcement personnel are more practical than legal. So long as they confine themselves to investigation and prosecution of federal crimes, there is no legal problem. The practical problem is whether their presence serves to aggravate the emotions of the populace or alienate local law enforcement officials. Marshals, in addition to problems of availability and training, would likely aggravate the problem. Increase of FBI personnel, along the lines previously followed, is not likely to have the same result and constitutes the most effective course of action that can be followed at the present time.

8

ANNELLE PONDER AND FANNIE LOU HAMER

Describing Events in Winona, Mississippi

1963

One of the myths surrounding the civil rights movement is that female activists were not subjected to police brutality. This document describes in detail what transpired when a group of black women, on their way home from a citizenship school in South Carolina, decided to desegregate a restaurant at a bus station in Winona, Mississippi. Annelle Ponder graduated from Clark College and was working with the Southern Christian Leadership Conference in the Delta. Teenager June Johnson had been brought into the movement by SNCC activists in Greenwood. Fannie Lou Hamer, a sharecropper evicted from her plantation after she attempted to register to vote, came to symbolize the grassroots movement in Mississippi. At the Democratic Convention in Atlantic City in 1964, a national television audience heard her tell the story of her arrest and beating.

MISS LEVINE: Describe what happened to you from the time you went into the bus station.
PONDER: Well, this is what happened. We left there, at Winona, at about 11:15 Sunday morning and then 3 or 4 of us got off the bus and went into the café to be served, and we sat down at the lunch counter and when we sat down there were 2 waitresses back of the counter and

SNCC Papers, reel 40, frames 452–57.

one of them just balled up her dish cloth, the wash cloth she had in her hand and threw it against the wall behind us. She said, "I can't take it no more," and so right after she said that the chief of police and highway patrol man came from the rear area of the café and came around and tapped us on the shoulder with billy clubs. Said "y'all get out, get out." We all stood up when he tapped us and when he got to me I said, "you know, it's against the law to put us out of here, don't you." He said, "ain't no damn law, you just get out of here." So we went on the outside and stood and talked about this for about 5 to 8 minutes and 2 other people, Euvester Simpson and Rosemary Freeman joined us out there. As I understand it, they had been in the restaurant. Euvester had tried to go to the rest room and one of the policemen had told her to go to a segregated one. He pointed out which one for her to go to, and so she came out and was telling us about that and we stood around talking for a few minutes. I went back to the door and looked in to get a better look at the patrolmen, the officers. They saw us looking in and then we came back out and stood and talked some more. We were just discussing it, what happened, and I said, well, we ought to get something and make a report on this, so then I happened to think the patrol car was right out there. So I said we could get the license plate number of the patrol car and we went around to the back to get this and as I was writing it down the patrolman and the chief of police came out of the restaurant. The chief of police said, "You're all under arrest, you're under arrest. Get in that car there." They had us get into the patrolman's car. As we were getting in the car Mrs. Hamer got off the bus and asked us if we wanted them to go on down to Greenwood. So I said yes, and then the chief of police hollered out, "get that one there, get that one there, bring her on down in the other car." So he got Mrs. Hamer and brought her on down—took us all down to the jail and when we got down there he didn't say what he charged us with. He said "you all are raising hell all over the place." And then they took us inside and had us standing up and starting asking some questions. Then they separated us, put some of us in the cell, and never did say what they were locking us up for. All of us were put in a cell except June Johnson; she was the last one out so they started talking to her and asking her questions. . . . And I could hear her say, "you all are supposed to protect us and take care of us." And after that I heard her screaming and we could hear the sounds of blows. They beat her a few minutes and then they came and got me out and sent her where I was and I passed her on the way out and she was bleeding in the face and she was crying. There was blood on the floor of the room where she had been and they told me to stand over there where she had been. So I went over and stood where she had been and they stood around about ½ a minute and then they started in asking me questions, started hitting me. One said to me "you all are down there stirring up shit and the more we stir the more it stank, you all were doing a demonstration." We were not, we had not planned a demonstration at all, we just went in there to eat, so we tried to explain this and they kept wanting me to say yes sir, "I want to hear you say, yes sir, nigger." Before they had separated us up in the cells, one officer in a blue uniform wanted to know if I had enough respect for him to say yes sir, and I told him I didn't know him that well. So he looked at me with a kind of amazed look, and after that they just kept trying to get me to say yes sir, and I would not and they kept hitting me, from one to the other and around, and this went on for about 10 minutes, talking and beating. I'd say there were at least 3, the highway patrolman, the blue-uniformed officer (I guess a local policeman), then there was a man who did not have a uniform, but he was a short man, but we saw him, he was there yesterday when we got out. I could identify him easily. One fellow, Squeaky, from down in Greenwood, has some good pictures we can use to identify them later on. Anyway, at least 3 of them kind of gave us the run over with black jacks, a belt, fists, open palm and at one point the highway patrolman hit me in the stomach. That went on off and on I guess about 10 minutes, talking and beating—they really wanted to make me say yes sir and that's one thing that I wouldn't say. . . .

JACK MINNIS: Please describe what happened from the time you were arrested on.

HAMER: It was the most horrifying experience I've ever had in my life. You see, I was on the bus, and Anelle and the others was off, part of the others was off the bus and when I saw the policemans carrying 'em to the car, and I know it wasn't going to be too long before we're supposed to be on our way to Greenwood I just stepped off and asked her what did she want us to do and she motioned for me to go on, that they would have to go down to the station. So by this time a man told me to wait and I stopped and he come round to the side of the car—it was 2 men in there, and he told me to come round there and get in, and when I went to get in, he kicked me (this was one of the officers). So I got in the car and he drove me round, just me. It was him and another person, so we went on round to the place where they had carried Miss Ponder and the others and after we had gotten there, wasn't too long before I heard some screaming, and I was in a cell then. It was one other girl with me, Euvester Simpson. She had been on the bus, he was one of them too. We was put in a room together. So they was asking, after I heard the hollering and going on and then I saw this girl pass the window where I could see her, then they had Miss Ponder. You know, that screaming and all of that will always follow me—I never will forget it and they whipped her, and after awhile she passed by where we was in the cell and her mouth was bleeding and her hair was standing up on her head and it was horrifying. So then after they decided to stop, well, this man asked me where I was from and I told him I was from Ruleville, so he said, well I'm going to check and see. And I figured well it wasn't going to be nothing happen to me because, I told him, I say, after all, I was born, I think it was, in this county, Montgomery County. He said, "and you stay in Ruleville now?" I say, yes sir. So he said, "well, I'm going to check, I'm going to see where you're from." So I know, you know, by me being one of the persons that works with this voter registration when he checked well that really was going to put me on the spot. So when he walked back in there he said, "yes, you live in Ruleville" and said "you the big . . ." and I've never heard that many names called a human in my life. He used all kinds of curse words. So one of the officers called me fatso, and then he said, "let's take her in here." So they carried me in a room and it was 2 Negro boys in this room. So the state highway patrol gave them a long blackjack and it was wide and he told one of the boys, said "take this." And he said, "this what you want me to use?" He said, "that's right" and said, "if you don't use it on her, you know what I'll use it on you." So then the boy told me to "get over there." I say, "where?" And he said, "on that cot." I said, "you mean you would do this to your own race?" Then this state patrolman said "you heard what I told you." He say, "all right, get over there and stretch out." So then I had to get over there on the bed, upside of my stomach and that man beat me, that man beat me til he give out, and by me screaming, made one of the other ones, a plain clothes fellow, he didn't have on nothing like a uniform, he got so hot and worked up off it, he just come there, you know, and started hitting on the back of my head. Well, my hands, I was trying to guard some of the licks, you see, my hands, they just beat my hands til they turned blue. And after he had finished, well my clothes, quite naturally, you know, beating me like that, my clothes come up and I tried to pull them down, you know, it was just pitiful. And then, one of the white fellows, one of the other white fellows, just take my clothes and snatched them up and this Negro when he had beat me til he was just, I know he was give out, well then this state patrolman told the other Negro to beat me, so he taken over from there. And he just beat me til, and anywhere you could see me you could see I'm not lying, because, you know, I just can sit down, I've been sleeping on my face and I was just hard as a bone. When they turned me loose I was hard as a bone. Then they carried me back to the cell. . . . There's something going to have to be done, it really is. You know now, what we get is give to us, me, you know me now. All right, my tax money goes just like anybody else, but still we don't have no protection. At the same time, mister, if it was your wife and you thought one small lick had been given, there would have been 1,050 soldiers there to protect that woman. But me, and I just don't know how long we can keep on going like this, and then after I got out of jail yesterday, half dead, to find out that Medgar Evers had been shot down in his own yard. Well, something got to break. And they just keep on saying wait and we been waiting all of our lives and still getting killed, still getting hung, still getting beat to death, now we're tired of waiting. Now ain't that right?

2

Organizing Freedom Summer

9

KU KLUX KLAN

Warning — Citizens of Ruleville

August 27, 1964

Although whites had been engaging in acts of violence and intimidation directed at black communities in Mississippi since the beginning of the civil rights movement, the Klan itself was not reborn until late 1963. Then, under the leadership of Imperial Wizard Sam Bowers, the White Knights of the Ku Klux Klan embarked on a reign of terror. Bowers gave the order to kill the three civil rights workers in Neshoba County at the beginning of Freedom Summer, hoping that this action would severely damage the summer project. It did not. As the summer progressed, the Klan grew increasingly frustrated over the failure of local white leaders to take drastic action against movement blacks and northern volunteers.

Warning Citizens of Ruleville

Our esteemed mayor, Charles M. Dorrough, Sr. backed by some of the town board — Hyman Turner, Gus Morgan, James Wooten, and J. M. Robertson, Jr. — has sold Ruleville to a pack of communistic, atheist, low moral punks from outside the boundaries of our beloved state.

These juvenile delinquents, beatniks, and prostitutes came to this community for one reason — to stir up and cause as much trouble as possible. And what did our mayor do? NOTHING! He even gave this scum

William Heath Research Papers, 1963–1997, State Historical Society of Wisconsin, Madison, Wis., box 5, folder 14. Hereafter cited, William Heath Papers.

police protection and when the police tried to do something he would not back them.

He has succumbed to their every whim, invited them out to dinner at the city's expense, and tried to help them succeed in their mission here.

Then the city board was approached by this group of outside punks and prostitutes with a demand of integrating our factories and setting up a school to train Negroes. The board immediately made arrangements with Yankee-Negro loving Prima[tes] to proceed with all speed to meet the demands of these outsiders.

Integration of public schools has come to our state and only forty miles away from our city—Clarksdale.

We have sat back and allowed punks and scum from outside the boundaries of our beloved southland to take away our cherished way of life in which both races have lived together in peace and harmony through the years.

These outsiders have been allowed the run of the county by many of our local politicians and have not even been offered token resistance. These politicians do not represent the general feeling of the citizens in our beloved community.

Our citizens have not been informed of their right to refuse giving any information to any FBI agent or Federal Marshal against his will. No efforts are being made to help organize private segregated schools so our children will not have to attend school with Negroes.

In order to preserve our way of life, our citizens must take a stand. We must protect our wives and children by banding together in an untiring effort to relieve our county of racial agitation and defeat from public office do-nothing politicians. Citizens of Ruleville, it is time we took another look at this bunch of FENCE-STRADDLING, PETTY POLITICIANS WE HAVE IN OFFICE.

Remember: INTEGRATION IS ONLY FORTY MILES AWAY
A LOCAL CIVIC GROUP

10

STUDENT NONVIOLENT
COORDINATING COMMITTEE

Meeting to Discuss Summer Project
January 24, 1964

Whether to invite hundreds of northern volunteers (most of whom, it was correctly assumed, would be white college students) was a topic hotly debated by COFO activists throughout the winter of 1963–1964. The issue had not yet been resolved in late January when SNCC activists met in Greenwood to discuss the summer project. Opposition to bringing down large numbers of whites came mostly from SNCC staff members who feared that black community leaders would retreat into the background once the volunteers arrived. Support came mostly from local people whose experience convinced them that their lives improved when outside organizers came to town. Which of the arguments advanced here do you find most persuasive?

Meeting, evening of January 24, 1964, to discuss summer project, Hattiesburg. Attending: Gwen Gillon, McArthur Cotton, Charles Sherrod, Sandra Hayden, Joyce Ladner, Willie Blue, Mike Sayer, Mendy Samstein, Lawrence Guyot, Frank Smith, Oscar Chase, Donna Moses, Joan Bowman, Jim Forman, Mrs. Ella Baker. Forman presided. George Greene, Helen O'Neal

Forman called for discussion of summer project.

Mrs. Baker reported on telephone call from Second Congressional District: They want no summer workers, especially for field; project "too difficult" to house and administer. In Greenville Carol Bolton opposed project because fears whites would take over project.

COTTON: Initially felt more time needed to "spell out" project; feels we still do not have enough time. However since recruitment is already under way, "will do all he can" for project. Main question is when we are ready.

SNCC Papers, reel 3, frames 829–30.

BOWMAN: Felt that staff apathy would mean failure. . . . Should be scuttled unless staff attitude changes.

GREENE: The staff has been forced into summer project; workers already recruited, without concrete commitment from staff. People on projects do not have enough opportunity to do creative things. . . .

SAMSTEIN: . . . Nothing resolved until December 15 staff meeting. Voted there to allow "unlimited number" of students. At later staff executive meeting decided to re-think question. Number defined as 100; at later meeting "verbal affirmation" to continue project. (His feelings) There will be a natural staff expansion: some outside projects will come such as the national council of churches. A broader program might be implemented by staff if "will" exists, with teams into counties, and workers into major cities.

HARRIS: At Greenville discussed notion of recruiting staff from state. Moses added students from out of state, thought in terms of 5,000. Voted, for them to come to do research-related work. Opposed until state executive meeting. At Tougaloo meeting Moses presented details of what they could do: freedom schools, community centers, research, voter registration. Agreed then because they would have something to do. Could create national attention. We voted to set up machinery; therefore we are committed.

HAYDEN: Idea is good because they get attention from congressmen, press. . . . Students should pay own way; we set up qualifications. Perhaps 100–500 could be absorbed. . . .

SMITH: Opposed the project from the beginning. Felt it was part of a pattern: not recruiting and developing state talent, instead taking easy way, using people who want to do "sociological research," then return to their campuses. To complete the revolution we must rethink. Feeling now is that we can learn from Hattiesburg Freedom Day and develop a program if we (1) recruit people (2) set up situation where they can work. In Columbus I can arrange housing and food; a number might be used for a "Freedom Day" there; would release energy. We have brought the people to a point, now they are ready for "something else." If summer project seen as moving people from one point to another, could utilize this energy. (Might take form of) demonstrations all over state, in every congressional district and by end of summer there will be no doubt that people in Mississippi want freedom. We can provide mechanism if we can orient students into projects.

GILLON: Bringing kids down would be good. Noted publicity which attended Freedom Vote. Could use them on voter registration.

D. MOSES: Opposed to any . . . to get publicity. If can orient around on-going program and if staff needed, then alright. Any staff must come for a meaningful length of time. . . .

LADNER: In favor of program if it can be developed to use people effectively. The freedom schools, community centers are meaningful and might be effective. They would be picked up doing voter registration. If we are not ready, then it should be thrown out now. Thousands are "in the clouds," should think in terms of hundreds.

SAYER: Fears that summer project might sink the Mississippi Project. Large numbers might overwhelm staff. We are having trouble with our own problems. Deplores tendency to think of organizing Mississippi "from outside" and the exaggerated focus on Washington. Do revolutions get organized from outside anywhere? . . .

BLUE: Notes the negative attitudes expressed, but thinks is a good project. The experience of having people, especially white, to "turn a friendly face" would be good, especially for kids. Doesn't see why it can't be done. "100 years too late."

CHASE: Does not agree that the summer project would inhibit Mississippi people and the Project. Ought to develop both. Kids will learn in Freedom Schools; Community Centers cause people to think about their conditions; does it matter that the people running these are from Peoria? . . . Hattiesburg shows that out of state people bring protection. We need federal government involved, and they never will move unless nation forces it to.

A. PONDER: (asked by Forman to contribute) Should be a state operation. Fit the students into current programs as district directors see it.

SHERROD: In favor of project, except can't go into it halfway. Might make or break us.

MRS. BAKER: Favors concept of summer program, as long as we can spell out what is possible and get to work on that. Having outside people who can offer leverage is good. Concern is that it adds to total thrust and growth of people involved. Those already working must map out program. Recruitment is important.

FORMAN: Must reach some consensus. There are two objectives: confrontation between state and federal governments, and the program for the students. Questions validity of notion of "cracking state" by summer project. . . .

SMITH: No specific program has been discussed, only some talk. Agrees with 3 objectives. Opposes "huge influx" or "crash program." In Columbus could use 30 students to develop classes for high school drop-outs, in Negro history, citizenship education, voter registration classes. Need staff to develop those programs. To work must knock on doors every day and have a responsible staff in charge. . . .

FORMAN: (citing paper on summer project drafted by 7–8 people) Suggests a discussion of the paper by topics.

- Office in Meridian: Suarez volunteered for job; Meridian was suggested because (1) tension free and (2) Suarez would not work elsewhere. Because of the advantages of office being in Jackson (COFO office with files, WATS line, other programs, central location) the consensus of group was to have office for summer project located in Jackson.

- Administrative Coordinator: . . . Decided to set up a steering committee: Gillon, Ladner, O'Neal, Hayden, Samstein, Morris, Mrs. Baker, which seems a good balance of white-black, north-south, those with administrative experience. Is to remain sufficiently flexible to add others. Hoped that someone will emerge to take overall responsibility. . . .

- Recruitment of northern students; Stipulation that students raise own money would relieve us of fund-raising. . . . There is some question about commitment of CORE and other COFO contributors to summer project. Pending that, we must assume the project is a SNCC project.

A general staff meeting on the summer project was suggested.

-End-

11

BOB MOSES

Speech on Freedom Summer at Stanford University
April 24, 1964

Bob Moses played a key role in the development of the Mississippi civil rights movement from the time of his first trip to the state in 1960 as a member of SNCC to his work on the reanimation and leadership of COFO. Deeply influenced by civil rights movement veterans like Ella Baker and Amzie Moore, Moses focused his energies on developing local leadership in an effort to win the right to vote and then to gain the political power necessary for black people to solve their own problems in their own ways. Moses was a central figure in developing and promoting the idea of the summer project within SNCC and around the nation. In this transcription of a speech he delivered on a college campus in advance of Freedom Summer, Moses explains his support of the project and also the challenges the project created among COFO staff members and community organizers. According to Moses, in what ways was Freedom Summer a political movement? What tensions did the project create among staff?

Now, for many of us, this will be a real turning point in terms of whether it will be possible to get anything out of the political structures that is meaningful in this country. I mean, we're trying to work as closely, and as assiduously, and as hard as we can within the political structures of this country. Trying to see if they will bend, if they have any flexibility, if they give at some point, if they can really accommodate themselves to the demands of the people. The problem, up to this point, is that they haven't bent. They haven't given. They haven't been able to come up with real solutions. Everything has been patchwork. And every time you put a patch on here, pressure mounts [there], and something explodes. And you put a patch on it there, and the pressure mounts here, and something else explodes. . . .

Robert P. Moses, "Speech on Freedom Summer at Stanford University," Palo Alto, Calif., April 24, 1964, *Say It Plain, Say It Loud,* American RadioWorks, http://americanradio works.publicradio.org/features/blackspeech/bmoses.html.

Well, I'd like to say just a little about the summer project, more concretely. And I'd like to do it in terms of some of the history of how it has evolved, and some of the problems which happened in the state as the conception of the summer project came about. The staff in Mississippi were violently opposed to the summer project when it was first announced. They were opposed to an invasion of white people coming in to do good, and to work for a summer, and to essentially run projects, they thought, without having any experience and basis for doing that. And we spent half of November, and all of December and January, and on into the very beginning of March, in very heated, tough discussions about what the summer project could be, what it couldn't be, what kind of hopes it held out for people in Mississippi and the country, and what it didn't, what were its limits, what were the things that really might happen . . . that would be significant?

And it was out of those discussions that we reached a very uneasy . . . but at least tentative agreement among the majority of the staff, to go ahead with concrete, specific programs. And to try and channel people who were coming down into very specific jobs and tasks. And it was out of that agreement that the idea and conception of freedom schools [came about], and doing something to try and break the psychological holds that Negroes have evolved and the concept of working in the community centers, and the concept of working in the white communities, the concept of trying to provide some cultural dimension to the program, and the concept to try to buttress and further the legal work group.

Now, on other hand, the people in Mississippi did not have the reaction of the staff at all. The farmers, and the people who live and work there, welcomed the whole idea. Because they feel that anybody who comes down to help is good. They need all the help they can get. [They feel] that they're isolated, that they're alone, that they have no real tools, that they face an overwhelming enemy, that any kind of help that they can get is welcome. So . . . it was this more than anything else that swayed a lot of us. Because . . . in many cases the instincts of the people, and particularly some of the rural farmers about these things are truer, deeper, less cluttered, and less bothered by personal problems, and things like that, than the instincts of . . . the staff and the people who are working. It was with this kind of background that we went into the project. And more and more as we've gotten into it, we've come to [the] consideration that the [volunteers] who come down should be under some very well established controls. That they should have some idea of some very significant things that they can do. But very limited [activities], and perhaps significant because they're limited. And that some of the things that we would try to do would not be some of the things that we first envisioned doing.

12

HOLLIS WATKINS

A Veteran Organizer Explains His Opposition to the Summer Project

1995

Hollis Watkins was among the first local leaders recruited into the movement by Bob Moses in 1961 when SNCC set up its first project in McComb. Watkins became a SNCC field secretary and worked around the state in Hattiesburg, Holmes County, Greenwood, and elsewhere. In 1964 he served as a project director for Holmes County and oversaw numerous volunteers during Freedom Summer. Later that summer, Watkins traveled to Atlantic City, where he worked as a staffer on the MFDP challenge at the Democratic National Convention. Watkins is also well known as a song leader who used music effectively as an organizing tool. Though a local person himself, Watkins had, by 1964, become more of an organizer, and he was among those who opposed the summer project. Why did Watkins oppose the summer project? What do you imagine caused Watkins to become a Freedom Summer project leader once the decision was made to move forward? What are the similarities and differences between the Moses and Watkins documents?

WATKINS: Well, one of the ways that it [Freedom Summer] would have been different is if it had been coordinated and based on the extent of local leadership development, the number of local people working and taking initiative in all of the various areas, [if] an assessment had been made in terms of numbers. Three people go to this community, seven people go to this county, ten people go to that project, one go

---

"An Oral History with Mr. Hollis Watkins, interviewer: John Rachal," vol. 670, Center for Oral History and Cultural Heritage of the University of Southern Mississippi, 1995.

to this one, five go here, in that manner, where that it would have clearly been a situation where that, that the local leadership would not have been overwhelmed and the extent of the young people coming in would not have been to the extent that they would have drawn on each other's energy, excitement, enthusiasm that led to the overrunning of local leadership, but would have been working under the guidance and direction *of* local leadership through that process. So that is kind of the way I saw it and felt it perhaps should have gone. It would have taken a little longer. . . .

RACHAL: That leads—that answer actually sort of leads into a question concerning the November '63 meeting where the discussion of Freedom Summer and the scale of white participation in Freedom Summer was discussed in heated form, from what I have read. And the arguments against a large-scale white infusion seemed to be somewhat along the lines that you just mentioned, namely that it could tend to displace the local leadership and shift the spotlight or the momentum from what people like you had been doing since '61 to a bunch of white Johnny-come-latelies who were there only for a summer and then to be gone. . . .

WATKINS: Well, those discussions, those debates definitely were heated and long. And I was one of those who was on the side of . . . not being for the influx of northerners. Now, in most cases, . . . people have taken it out of the context and really made it an influx . . . of whites. But at that particular time, it was *not* really the black-white issue as much as it was the north-south issue. It was our opinion that, number one, people from the North, be they black or white, felt that they were better than us from the South. And with that attitude existing then we knew that the minute they came they would automatically attempt to take over and run things. The other thing we felt is that by them taking over, or attempting to take over, that would automatically bring about friction between them and local people. In some cases, depending on who the people would be, they might confront it but also because of partially submissiveness and part of not trying to do anything that would hurt or affect the overall good, black people might . . . just sit back and let you run with it. But we [also] felt that with young people coming in who had no knowledge of the South and Mississippi, this would be very dangerous. . . . And we also understood and felt that these young people would be on a fast-track. And we also understood that that was natural, because they were recruited based on coming to Mississippi and spending a summer and if you are coming somewhere to work, and if your heart is right, you're interested in doing as much as you can, as fast as you can over that short period of time. And in many cases based on what we were doing, speed was the wrong approach. So all of this, we felt, would bring about conflict and was not the appropriate thing to do. And based on those and other reasons, we felt that we should not have an influx of young northerners coming down to Mississippi, as we would say, taking over the movement and, in many cases, changing the course of direction, and after three or four or five months, be gone. When the dust settles, we the Mississippians would be left to sweep up the particles and try to recollect them and get them set back on the right course. We also felt that this kind of action would *seriously* thwart the initiative that black local leaders were just beginning to develop and take. So those were some of the things that we felt.

RACHAL: In retrospect and with the hindsight of thirty-two years, what do you think about Freedom Summer? Do you think you were right? Basically I'm asking you do you think in retrospect that you were right, or maybe not right, or what is your view on this very same question from the perspective of thirty-two years later?

WATKINS: From the perspective of thirty-something years later, my perspective is [that] we were right. . . . Not saying that a lot wasn't accomplished and came out of it, even though a lot was accomplished, a lot of good was done—I still think we were right.

13

COUNCIL OF FEDERATED ORGANIZATIONS

Guidelines for Interviewing

1964

Once COFO decided to invite hundreds of college students to spend the summer in Mississippi, support groups in the North began interviewing potential volunteers. This document includes specific criteria for evaluating each applicant. During the freedom vote, northern students created some problems; thus COFO leaders wanted to weed out applicants who might inadvertently cause trouble. If you were applying for the summer project, would you have met the standards?

Alicia Kaplow Papers, 1964–1968 Archives, Main Stacks, State Historical Society of Wisconsin, Madison, Wis., box 1, folder 4.

During the Freedom Vote for Governor campaign in the fall of 1963 over seventy Yale and Stanford students came to Mississippi. Since these volunteers were in the state for no more than a week, there was no opportunity to make extensive evaluation of their ability to adjust to movement conditions in Mississippi. But one strong observation can be drawn from their participation. The great majority of students came down with the attitude—"I know I am only going to be here for a very short period of time, but I am willing to help in whatever way you think I can." There were some students, however, who came to Mississippi with fixed ideas about what they wanted to do and what they hoped to achieve. A case study might best illustrate this attitude.

One student arriving in Jackson received initial authorization to go to Yazoo City, a hard-core town, where in the past civil rights workers had been driven out. He was sent to Canton to discuss plans for this move with the project director there. The project director, however, viewing his entire area and its work needs, felt that a move into Yazoo City at the time would be ill-advised. The student became extremely argumentative and repeatedly insisted on being taken to Yazoo City. The project director became so harassed he called Jackson for assistance and was advised to bring the student back to Jackson. In Jackson, several of the members of the staff leadership tried to explain the importance of abiding by decisions of the local staff head; the student, however, continued to argue and insist that he be permitted to go to Yazoo City. Since no one could reason with him, it was decided that he should remain in Jackson until it was time for him to leave the state.

This case study should give the interviewer a general idea of one criterion, and perhaps the most important one, for evaluating applicants. If the problem presented by the above student were multiplied enough times (there will be almost a thousand volunteers in Mississippi this summer) the whole program could be jeopardized and lives could even be lost.

A few more general observations can be made:

The lack of experience in civil rights activity or in the South need not (and should not) be considered grounds for disqualifying an applicant. (This should be clear from the size of the project being undertaken in Mississippi this summer.) But it is essential that an applicant possess a learning attitude toward work in Mississippi. This is not to discourage ingenuity or creativity; it means that an applicant must have some understanding that his role will only be a stopgap one: that the movement will have to continue after he leaves and that his role will be to *work with* local leadership, not to *overwhelm* it. He can only do this if he shows some respect for what has gone before him and an understanding of what must continue after he leaves. He must be capable of understanding that the success of the Mississippi movement depends on the development of those who live and will remain in the state. A student who seems determined to carve his own niche, win publicity and glory when he returns home can only have harmful effects on the Mississippi program.

There are other criteria which should guide the Mississippi Summer Project interviewers. . . .

1. Experience and training in teaching or community work will be of great value to the project.

2. Special skills (e.g. in the arts, in health care, in communication) would be similarly valuable.

3. A basic sense that the civil rights movement (not just abstract justice) is a good thing.

4. A willingness to admit doubts and fears about going to Mississippi.

5. An understanding of the risks involved in working in Mississippi—jail, possible beatings, etc. (Under Mississippi political conditions it would be impossible to assure an individual working even in a "safe situation" that he will not be arrested.)

6. Some understanding of the living conditions they will have to work under in Mississippi, i.e. the fact that they will be living in homes and sharing food with people who are extremely poor.

7. Excessive nervousness (if such can be detected in an interview) would be a hazard to the applicant as well as to others under Mississippi conditions.

8. Extremely dogmatic and ideological views would probably be a detriment to the project. Mississippi has real problems which must be approached and understood empirically.

Further, interviewers should be on guard for those who take an apocalyptic view toward the Mississippi summer program—the struggle for political and social justice in Mississippi will not reach a conclusion as a result of this summer.

Final note: The above criteria are those which we thought would be meaningful in interviewing people for civil rights work in Mississippi. We did not believe it would be useful to list criteria which most interviewers would apply anyway (e.g. emotional maturity, responsibility). Finally, interviewers have been left to formulate their own questions for the purpose of eliciting pertinent responses from applicants.

14

COUNCIL OF FEDERATED ORGANIZATIONS

Application Form for Andrew Goodman
1964

Many more people applied to work in Mississippi than were accepted. The application below was submitted by Andrew Goodman, the volunteer who, along with James Chaney and Michael Schwerner, was murdered by Klan members during the first week of the summer project. What do the questions on the application tell you about the kind of volunteer COFO was looking for? What do we learn about Andrew Goodman from his application?

Mississippi Summer Project

Name *Andrew Goodman*   Age *20*

Address *161 W 86 St N.Y.C.*

Occupation *Student - Queens College*

Business Address _____

List your hometown and city newspapers

New York Times

(name)   (address)

New York Herald Tribune

National Guardian   *197 E 4th St N.Y. N.Y. 10009 -Weekly*

The Nation   *333 Sixth Ave N.Y. N.Y 10014 -Weekly*

List the organizations to which you belong

(name)	(officer)	(address)

List your Senators

Jacob K. Javits   *Republican*
(name)   (party)

Kenneth B. Keating   *Republican*

Congressman:

William Fitts Ryan   *Democrat*
(name)   (party)

Describe briefly the civil rights activities you have participated in.

March to Washington - Summer 1963

   "   " *- Three previous marches*

Given Contributions

If you have ever been arrested, give place, date, charge, and status of case.

List any contact who could be helpful in securing your release from jail if you are arrested or who could help with publicity about your activities.

Ralph Engelman 62-36 86ᵗʰ St Elmhurst N.Y.

- Has Grant from Newspaper Fund Inc.

- Not sure yet of Periodical

List any other persons who should be notified if you are arrested or harassed.

Robert W Goodman - 161 W 86 St New York City

Please number your choices of the work you would like to do in Mississippi.

_5_ Community Centers _2_ Research

_3_ Freedom Schools _6_ White Communities

_1_ Voter Registration _7_ Legal

_4_ Communications (press relations, photography, etc.)

Describe briefly your qualification (training and/or experience) for your first choice.

I am a Junior at Queens College majoring in Anthropology. My schooling so far has been oriented towards history and I have a good knowledge of current affairs. Finally I have a good deal of experience with racial and religious prejudice in the North and South.

Check the skills you have:

_____ Journalism	_____ Music	_____ Library Science
_____ Art	_____ Photography	_____ Nursing
_✓_ Dramatics	_✓_ Research	_____ Recreation

Check the subjects you could teach:

_✓_ Literacy	_✓_ Literature
_✓_ Remedial reading and writing	_____ Hygiene
_✓_ English	_____ Home Economics
_____ Math	_____ Federal Programs
_____ Political Science	_____ Auto Mechanics
_____ Negro History	_____ Typing
_____ Foreign Language	_____ Shorthand

I can _✓_ drive a car

_____ type _____ words a minute

_____ work office machinery

I have a driver's license from the state of _____ New York _____

Do you have a car you could use during your time in Miss.? ~~Yes~~ No

I will be able to work in Mississippi from _July_ until _September_

I will be able to be self-supporting (roughly $150) _____ ✓ _____

15

COUNCIL OF FEDERATED ORGANIZATIONS

Security Handbook

1964

COFO sent out several letters to the volunteers who had been accepted into the program, including information about the Oxford orientation, the resources the volunteers needed to bring to Mississippi, and the books they were assigned to read. The "Security Handbook," a comprehensive list of dos and don'ts for the volunteers, is based on the collective experiences of the veteran movement activists.

Communications personnel will act as security officers.

Travel

a. When persons leave their project, they *must* call their project person to person for *themselves* on arrival at destination point. Should they be missing, project personnel will notify the Jackson office. WATS line operators will call each project every day at dinnertime or thereabouts, and should be notified of changes in personnel, transfers, etc. . . . Checklists should be used in local projects for personnel to check in and out.

b. Doors of cars should be locked at all times. At night, windows should be rolled up as much as possible. Gas tanks must have locks and be kept locked. Hoods should also be locked.

c. No one should go *anywhere* alone, but certainly not in an automobile, and certainly not at night.

d. Travel at night should be avoided unless absolutely necessary.

e. Remove all unnecessary objects from your car which could be construed as weapons. (Hammers, files, iron rules, etc.)

Jerry Tecklin Papers, 1964, Archives Main Stacks, MSS 538, State Historical Society of Wisconsin, Madison, Wis., box 1, folder 5.

Absolutely no liquor bottles, beer cans, etc. should be inside your car. Do not travel with names and addresses of local contacts.

   f. Know all roads in and out of town. Study the county map.

   g. Know locations of sanctuaries and safe homes in the county.

   h. When getting out of a car at night, make sure the car's inside light is out.

   i. Be conscious of cars which circle offices or Freedom Houses. Take license numbers of all suspicious cars. Note make, model and year. Cars without license plates should immediately be reported to the project office.

Living at Home or in Freedom Houses

   a. If it can be avoided, try not to sleep near open windows. Try to sleep at the back of the house, i.e., the part farthest from a road or street.

   b. Do not stand in doorways at night with the light at your back.

   c. At night, people should not sit in their rooms without drawn shades.

   d. Do not congregate in front of the house at night.

   e. Make sure doors to Freedom Houses have locks, and are locked.

   f. Keep records of suspicious events, i.e., the same car circling around the house or office several times during the day or week. . . .

   g. If an "incident" occurs, or is about to occur, call the project, and then notify local FBI and police.

   h. Depending on project needs and circumstances, it may be advisable for new personnel to make deliberate attempts to introduce themselves immediately to local police and tell them their reason for being in the area.

   i. A phone should be installed in each Freedom House, if there isn't one already. . . .

Personal Actions

   a. Carry identification at all times. Men should carry draft cards.

   b. All drivers should have in their possession driver's licenses, registration papers, and bills of sale. The information should also be on record with the project director. If you are carrying supplies, it might be well to have a letter authorizing the supplies from a particular individual to avoid charges of carrying stolen goods.

c. Mississippi is a dry state and though liquor is ostensibly outlawed, it is available everywhere. You *must not* drink in offices, or Freedom Houses. This is especially important for persons under 21.

d. Try to avoid bizarre or provocative clothing, and beards. Be neat.

e. Make sure that prescribed medicines are clearly marked, with your name, the doctor's name, etc.

Relations with the Press

a. Refer questions about SNCC's perspective or policies to the Project Director.

b. Do not argue with the press. Do not exaggerate. Give the facts only. . . .

c. Try to relate your activities to the lives of the local residents. This will not be hard to do, or unnatural, if you remember your role in the state.

Information to Police

Under no circumstances should you give the address of the local person with whom you are living, his or her name, or the names of any local persons who are associated with you. When police ask where you live, give your local project or Freedom House address, or if necessary, your out of state address.

Relations with Visitors

Find out who strangers are. If persons come into project offices to "look around" try to discover who they are and what exactly they want to know. All offers of assistance should be cleared through the project director.

Records

1. Any written record of importance should have at least four copies. Keep original, send copies to Jackson, Greenwood, and Atlanta. Bear in mind that the office might be raided at any time.

2. Keep a record of interference with phone lines and of notifications of FBI. . . .

Policy

1. People who do not adhere to disciplinary requirements will be asked to leave the project.
2. Security precautions are a matter of group responsibility. Each individual should take an interest in every other person's safety, well-being, and discipline.
3. At all times you should be aware of the danger to local residents. White volunteers must be especially careful.

16

COUNCIL OF FEDERATED ORGANIZATIONS

Letter to Freedom School Teachers

1964

Organizers of the freedom schools knew that most of the volunteers teaching in the program lacked classroom experience. These documents show that the freedom school teachers had more "homework" to do than the other volunteers and that they were expected to bring most of their teaching materials, including blackboards and chalk, with them to Mississippi.

---

1. *Each Freedom School teacher must bring with him:*(These are small items without which the Freedom Schools cannot operate and which you can purchase or secure easily by soliciting them or the funds with which to buy them.) *At least*:

   1 quire four hole stencils (A.B. Dick or Gestetner)

   1 typewriter, typing paper, carbon paper

Hank Werner Papers, State Historical Society of Wisconsin, Madison, Wis., box 1, folder 1.

25 pencils
25 ball point pens
25 pads lined paper (preferably legal size)
5 magic markers (for making visual aids and signs)
1 pair scissors
roll scotch tape
package thumb tacks
stapling machine and staples
paper clips
1 item sports equipment
first aid kit

In addition, each person who has a special skill area (from teaching remedial math to leading modern dance classes to teaching an arts-crafts skill) *must* bring all the materials he will need. Each teacher should choose one or more activities he could lead or teach as a specialty and bring materials to set up that program.

Finally, when you receive and read the *Curriculum Guide* you will find numerous suggestions for visual aids, books, etc. We cannot count on supplying *any* of these materials. . . .

2. Each Freedom School teacher should *try to bring with him*: (or send to address below if you can secure in quantity)

    blackboards, chalk   dictionary
    bulletin boards   prints of artistic works
    camera and film
    maps—world, U.S., Mississippi

    books that would interest high school students, especially that require low reading levels or that center on Negro history and thought

17

VINCENT HARDING

Freedom Summer Orientation Briefing
1964

Dr. Vincent Harding was asked by the organizers of Freedom Summer to address the volunteers at the Oxford, Ohio, orientation sessions. A nonviolent Mennonite, Harding was a civil rights and peace activist, a theologian, and a historian. He was at the center of much civil rights activity. He was a close adviser to Dr. Martin Luther King and was also close to many student activists. Harding's purpose was to prepare the volunteers to meet the kinds of people who lived in Mississippi—organizers and local people, white and black, rural and urban, educated and illiterate, open to the movement and hostile to it. In this selection from his briefing, he openly addresses the deep caverns of race and region that separated white from black, and he touches on the intersectional points of race, sex, gender, and age. If you had been a summer volunteer, how would you have reacted to Dr. Harding's presentation?

I want to start out first by saying that those of us who have been talking about this project for six or eight months have always talked about it with a good deal of apprehension. And a part of the apprehension has grown out of the fact that we didn't quite know what kind of kooks would be coming down to take part in this revolution. . . . But from what I can see, I think that a great many persons who talked about this over the difficult winter and the spring . . . have seen you here at Oxford, have had a great sense of encouragement by your presence. . . .

When the Supreme Court declared against segregation in 1954, it declared that it was unconstitutional because it was unjust. With that declaration a new age began in America, the age of racial revolution. . . .

When the nation's highest tribunal condemned the unjust wall of segregation, we could no longer hide. . . .

Vincent Harding, "Freedom Summer Orientation Briefing," 1964, Civil Rights Movement Veterans, www.crmvet.org/docs/harding.htm.

So a strange revolution developed, a revolution in which the Negroes in the South, and increasingly in the North, were committed to overthrowing the existing illegal, unjust system of segregation in favor of the constitutional system of desegregation and justice. . . .

The wall was high and hard and many lives had been lost against it. And more and more persons were growing bitter and impatient. Not simply against the wall itself, but against the millions of Americans who by their apathy and passive cooperation allowed it to stand. So they challenged Martin Luther King asking, "Why? Why do we have to love? Why do we have to love, even after beatings, and rejections, and deaths? Why?"

You will meet men and women in Mississippi that are asking that question. And I would like to fold this over with three approaches to what you will meet in Mississippi. Something about the black men that you will meet who have come out of this history, something about the white men that you will meet that have come out of this history, and something about how you might possibly respond to these men and women who shall not be known unless you know out of what they have come.

There are black men who say "why" in Mississippi, for there is a bitterness deep within them that must not be denied. It must not be encouraged, but it must not be denied. A bitterness against their white rulers, a bitterness against the white man. You hear it again and again. You have heard it here many times. The "white man." There are dangers involved in calling people the "white man," calling people the "redneck" for these stereotypes are just as dangerous as the "Negro," and the "colored" man. But men and women live within these stereotypes as a result of their history. Whether you like it or not, you are the white man to many of them.

Therefore as you meet them, you shall meet them with them having very mixed feelings about you. Make no bones about that. For they will meet you with gladness and with fear. They will meet you with hope and with distrust. Let me give you an example. The staff people who are in Mississippi . . . many of them have not known the kind of college experiences that you have known. Therefore when you come into the meetings; when you come with all of your well articulated ideas; when you come with all of your high flung theory about how it should be done; when you come with all of the answers one through ten, quickly written up on the blackboard, they will hate your guts.

In spite of the fact that they know that some of these things may be right, they will still hate you because they cannot speak in the same way, because they cannot think with the same kind of accuracy, because they cannot move with the same kind of objectivity. And you must go recognizing that this is how they will feel. They have known white folks being in charge for a long, long time. And it is impossible for many of them now to believe that any white folk could possibly be qualified to be in charge. And so . . . they will know deeply within themselves that you have the qualifications in many situations to be in charge, but they will not want you to be in charge. And they will not let you be in charge. . . .

They are going to do it. . . . You will meet a strange mixture of love and hate as a result of this kind of history. . . . You are going to find it as I say in a certain kind of sexual aggressiveness, both in the form of Negro fellows and Negro girls towards you. It grows out of the love/hate response, but it grows out of some other things. It grows out of that curiosity which is inevitable when people have lived on opposite sides of walls. And not only are they curious, but obviously you are curious too. . . . And you are going to have to determine how you are going to meet this. Unfortunately some people think that the only way that a white person can prove that they are with the movement is to go to bed with a Negro. You will have to deal with this. And you will have to deal with it quite honestly. . . .

You will meet them and you will have, I think, a strange kind of reaction to them. Because these will be the Negroes of Mississippi who out of the habit of generations of survival techniques will always be agreeing with you. Nothing that you say will be wrong. They will never be honest with you, and therefore they will never be able to be human with you, until they are able to be honest with you. But underneath their "yes siring" and "no Ma'aming" and "sure that is right," there will be a deep distrust, and probably a hatred of you because they have to act this way towards you. You will meet that. And there will be some people who will be very upset about it.

An example. You will go out some of you with Negroes to help recruit people for the Freedom Schools or for the community centers. And when you and the Negro walk into this Negro's house again and again and again this Negro will be looking at you and talking to you and saying, "Yes sir, yes ma'am, that is right." And paying no attention at all to the Negro that has walked in with you. That Negro is going to be pretty angry with you as a result of that. You must realize that this is the case.

You will be meeting of course Negroes whose spirits may not be quite broken, but who are very much afraid. Who are afraid, and who are seeking at any costs to stay on good terms with white people. And they will stay on good terms with any white people that they can find, you see. Then this is going to be hard for you. And I am going to say a little bit later on about how I think it might be dealt with. But recognize that it is going to be there.

But thank God you are going to meet some other Negroes too, some that you have already met here. You are going to meet some that have been freed, and some that are in the process of being freed. You are going to meet some who have been freed in their old age, and who are some of the great saints of this movement. You are going to be living in the house with some of them, as a matter of fact; who could not be having you in their house unless they were freed, unless they were somehow able to even transcend their history.

And you will be meeting these people who are determined to act out their freedom in every aspect of life and you must stand beside them and walk beside them. For these, some of them have even been freed from the need to hate, which is one of the greatest freedoms of all. . . . Well, I would say when you find these kind hold them tightly. Or more likely when they find you, hold them tightly because they are souls of great price.

Let me say a bit about the whites that you will meet. It is impossible to imagine that this kind of history could have been lived by white persons without, well, without a certain kind of national mental illness being involved. Bob Moses calls it the plague, perhaps that is as good as any term. From what I have seen among those who are white in the state of Mississippi, the best single word that could be used to characterize their condition at this moment especially is fear. I want you to really understand this. And I won't get you to understand this in five minutes of course, but I hope that you will try.

It is a fear approaching paranoia. And indeed it probably is a kind of paranoia. Because for a long time Mississippi has lived in a state that has encouraged paranoia from within and without. Everything threatens many of the white people of Mississippi. Everything that is new, everything that is strange, everything from a Negro voting to a white girl in a hip-length shift dress. Anything that is new threatens the white Mississippian. For everybody is against them you see. The whole nation is against them, the United Nations is against them, the world is against them. And they are fighting a lonely, noble battle as they understand it. In many cases this fear is the predominant feeling. And remember, I think if you remember this fear I think it will have something to do with how you approach people who are caught by fear even more than they are caught by hatred. . . .

And you know when you sing, "I am not afraid, I am not going to let the Ku Klux Klan turn me around, or the White Citizens Council," to a large degree the Klan and the Citizens Councils isn't mostly worried about the Negro in Mississippi, or even those of us who come to work with the Negroes of Mississippi. The Klan and the White Citizens Councils are worried about the other white people of Mississippi. And these white people in Mississippi live under constant fear of these organizations. . . .

Because of this fear, and because of this history, there is a tremendous sense of threat about Negroes achieving political power. . . . [Senator

James] Eastland and [Senator John C.] Stennis and a number of other people are saying . . . "But my goodness in counties where the Nigras are 60 or 70 percent of the population, how can we let them get into political power?" They are afraid. And of course you know why they are afraid. They are afraid because they know what happened when whites were in control of the Negro minority. Therefore, they can't imagine that they think that hell could result when the Negro gets in control of the political situation. . . .

But the final thing that I would say about the whites that you will meet is that you will meet some white people in Mississippi, believe it or not, who have not been backed up against the wall; . . . who have not allowed themselves to lose their humanity through fear. Some people will tell you that there are no such white people in Mississippi. All I can say is that I know that there are. And you had better look for them because Mississippi will not change until there are white people who are working with Negroes to change it.

How does one deal with this? I am not sure. . . . I think we have to recognize that we are dealing with a situation that is somewhat out of keeping with our American way of life at this point. Because we have now, especially in our generation, we have now moved into the cruel world, in which men say there are no ideologies, there are no causes. . . . And so we are going into Mississippi for a cause in the midst of a society that doesn't believe in causes except the saving of one's own skin. I think that we had better recognize that we are not going to be heroes. . . .

I would say, just as a general policy, be somewhat hesitant at first to throw out too many ideas at once. . . . Remember that most of you are going to be there for six, or seven, or eight quick hot weeks. And therefore, the important thing must never become your ideas. The important thing must become the ability of the people who you are leaving there to struggle through with their own. And if you are throwing out your own all the time they are not going to have much of an opportunity to develop leaders. . . .

We are going to Mississippi for one thing because men in this country have spent a long time using other men for their purposes. Remember that. That has been one of the troubles. Men and women have used other men and women as things, as objects, to get what they want. Now the question is if we are going to fight in a struggle against this kind of thing, against men using other people, then can we go and fight in that struggle and at the same time be involved ourselves in using other people. . . .

On this matter of how you respond to black racism, all I can say is, well, recognize where it comes from . . . recognize that black racism is there because of your white racism. And recognize that no matter how many times you come to Mississippi you are probably bringing some along with you. And you have to admit this. . . .

On the broken spirits that you are going to meet there. Please, as much as you can possibly do it with honesty and courtesy do not let them treat you the way that they treat Mr. Charlie. Do not let them scrape to you. Do not let them be dishonest with you. . . . Because the more that you let them go on in this kind of pattern, the more that you are killing them. . . . For the Negroes that you meet that have been freed, think very seriously about what they have gone through to be free. . . . And at every moment have a deep concern for their feelings, for their opinions, and a respect for their safety. And remember, please, that they have been living there, and that they are going to be living there when we get back to the white, free, liberal North. . . .

They have already in a sense risked everything to have you there. Because after you move out of that house it may be less than a few days later that there will be no more house. It may not happen while you are in there. . . .

I was going to say something about how to deal with the white fears but I won't because we can talk about that in the discussions after the break. Except to remind you again that what you are facing is fear. Fear is not overcome by threats, fear is not overcome by defiance, fear is not overcome by the promising of more. Fear is never gotten rid of that way. Until we find ways of dealing with their fear we are not going to beat Mississippi.

18

ROBERT F. KENNEDY

Memorandum for the President on Expected Violence and Lawlessness in Mississippi

May 21, 1964

A major problem facing the White House concerning the situation in Mississippi was that the FBI under J. Edgar Hoover had not provided useful intelligence. Assistant Attorney General for Civil Rights Burke Marshall made a trip to Mississippi to see for himself. His report is the basis for this memorandum from Attorney General Kennedy to President Johnson. Kennedy considered "the situation in Mississippi to be very dangerous," discussed the threats posed by white extremist groups like the Ku Klux Klan, and suggested that the president ask Hoover and the FBI to take a more active role in identifying terrorist groups and individuals in Mississippi.

This week at my request Burke Marshall spent some time in Southwestern Mississippi and Jackson to get some first-hand impressions of the possibilities for this summer and the future. He has reported the following general conclusions to me:

1. There has unquestionably been, as you know, an increase in acts of terrorism in this part of Mississippi. As a result the tensions are very great not only between whites and Negroes, but among whites. This is not as true in Jackson as in the outlying areas.

2. Law enforcement officials, at least outside of Jackson, are widely believed to be linked to extremist anti-Negro activity, or at the very least to tolerate it. There appears to be sound basis for this in many places. For example, groups have been formed under the auspices of the Americans for the Preservation of the White Race, to act as deputized law enforcement officials in some counties. A spot check shows that such groups are undergoing a

---

Memo, Robert F. Kennedy to the President, May 21, 1964, "Ex HU 2 3/26/64–5/24/64," WHCF, box 2, LBJ Library.

sort of training program in Walthall, Amite, Adams and Leake Counties. Every indication is that this is a very limited list. These groups appear to include individuals of the type associated with Klan activities. . . .

3. The area is characterized by fear based upon rumor. In Jackson rumors of organized Negro attacks on whites appear to be deliberately planted and spread in an organized fashion through pamphlets, leaflets, and word of mouth. The acceptance of these rumors as fact increases the hold that extremist white organizations have over events in most of the area.

It seems to me that this situation presents new and quite unprecedented problems of law enforcement.

As one step I am directing some of the personnel here in the Department who have had organized crime experience to make a more detailed survey of the area to try to substantiate the details concerning the activities of extremist groups, to trace the source of rumors and to develop facts concerning the acts of terrorism which are at least generally believed to have taken place in the last few weeks.

In addition, it seems to me that consideration should be given by the Federal Bureau of Investigation to new procedures for identification of the individuals who may be or have been involved in acts of terrorism, and of the possible participation in such acts by law enforcement officials or at least their toleration of terrorist activity. . . .

The unique difficulty that seems to me to be presented by the situation in Mississippi (which is duplicated in parts of Alabama and Louisiana at least) is in gathering information on fundamentally lawless activities which have the sanction of local law enforcement agencies, political officials, and a substantial segment of the white population. The techniques followed in the use of specially trained, special assignment agents in the infiltration of Communist groups should be of value. If you approve, I recommend taking up with the Bureau the possibility of developing a similar effort to meet this new problem. It might be desirable to ask for a report to you by the end of the month giving in detail what information the Bureau has been able to develop in the various counties of Mississippi on the members and leadership of any Klan group and of the Americans for the Preservation of the White Race, or any similar organizations, as well as their present activities and plans for the immediate future.

I told you in our meeting yesterday that I considered the situation in Mississippi to be very dangerous. Nothing in the reports I have received since then changes my view on that point.

19

LEE WHITE

Memorandum for the President on Missing Civil Rights Workers

June 23, 1964

In this memo, presidential aide Lee White informs President Johnson of the news that three civil rights workers had gone missing. He tells the president that CORE leader James Farmer and New York congressman William Fitts Ryan have some doubts about the urgency of the FBI's response to the disappearance. Racial violence in Mississippi was commonplace in this period, and few incidents of this kind reached the level of a presidential briefing. Based on the memo, why do you imagine this incident reached the president's desk? Why would a New York congressman be interested in this incident?

Yesterday morning at about 11:30 James Farmer of CORE called to advise that three of "their people" had been missing since Sunday morning at 9:00 a.m. The three were Mike Schwerner, Andrew Goodman and James Chayney [*sic*], the last a Negro. They had departed from Meridian for Philadelphia, Mississippi, 37 miles away. Apparently there were conflicting reports as to whether the three had been arrested for speeding on Sunday evening. One report had it that they had been arrested and released at 10:30 p.m. Sunday night. In any event, they were reasonable and well trained individuals who would have been in contact with their Meridian office by telephone.

Farmer had talked to John Doar at the Justice Department and had been assured that the FBI would do everything possible to find the young men. Mr. Farmer called here for purposes of notification and to urge our assistance in any way possible. I advised him that I would be in touch with Justice to be sure that everything possible was being done. I then called Burke Marshall who informed me that they were well aware of what was going on and that the FBI was cooperating fully.

Memo, Lee White to the President, June 23, 1964, attached to note, Lee White to the President, June 29, 1964, "Ex HU 2/ST 24 1/1/64–7/15/64," WHCF, box 26, LBJ Library.

Farmer called again late in the afternoon to say that his information was that there appeared to be no activity on the highway between Meridian and Philadelphia. He did, however, suggest that there was a Naval Air Station within seven miles of Meridian that might have equipment that could be used in a search. I relayed this to Burke Marshall who got in touch with the Navy and the equipment was made available to the FBI. The last information that I had at 8:00 last night was that a full scale search was on.

At 12:00 last night Congressman Ryan tried to call the President and finally got in touch with me. He wanted to be sure that this matter had been brought to our attention and to indicate that word had reached him that the FBI and Federal government generally were not particularly aggressive in their efforts to find the three boys. I assured him that my information was to the contrary, that we were as anxious to find them as he believed he was and told him that any specific suggestions and recommendations that he had would be most welcome.

> Lee C. White
> Associate Special Counsel
> to the President

Mrs. Juanita Roberts:

I assume the President might want to glance at this before I put it in the files.

> Lee C. White
> June 23, 1964

20

LEE WHITE

Memorandum for the President concerning a Request by Parents of the Missing Civil Rights Workers to Meet with the President

June 23, 1964

As this memorandum to President Johnson makes clear, the parents of missing activists Michael Schwerner and Andrew Goodman were coming to Washington and wanted to meet with the president. Note the cautious tone adopted by Lee White. Why did he see this visit as a potential political problem for the Johnson administration?

The parents of Andrew Goodman and Mike Schwerner are coming to Washington from New York City. . . . Both Congressmen Bill Ryan and Ogden Reid have urged strongly that you meet with these parents even if for a moment. Moreover, I am advised by Ryan that the New York press is aware of the fact that he has attempted to arrange a meeting with you.

Although very little can be done that is not already being accomplished by the FBI, it seems to me that there is a legitimate reason for seeing these people for a moment or two. First is the natural concern and anxiety that all will feel (especially parents) by way of sympathy for these people whose children are in serious straits. Secondly, it will dramatize the fact that everything that can be done by the Federal Government is now being undertaken.

On the other hand, since their trip to Washington is being highly publicized and the fact that they have sought a Presidential meeting, there could be a negative reaction if it appears that the Government is only casually interested or lukewarm in its efforts to find these young people. . . .

Memo, Lee White to the President, June 23, 1964, attached to note, Lee White to the President, June 29, 1964, "Ex HU 2/ST 24 1/1/64–7/15/64," WHCF, box 26, LBJ Library.

Should you meet with them, it would not be necessary to endorse the project, to blame Mississippi or to do anything other than express personal concern and assurance that every proper action will be taken to find these people.

21

CLARIE COLLINS HARVEY

Mississippi Summer Project— Womanpower Unlimited

August 15, 1964

Some of the strongest local support for the movement in the black community came from an organization called Womanpower Unlimited. Jackson businesswoman Clarie Collins Harvey founded it in the spring of 1961 as a support group for the freedom riders who were arrested in Jackson and later sent to Parchman Penitentiary. This document illustrates how local people, and black women in particular, provided an infrastructure for community organizing to flourish.

Historian Tiyi Morris refers to the role of the women in this organization as "other mothering." What did she mean, and why would a program like Freedom Summer require "other mothering"? The activism of Womanpower Unlimited points to the significant role that women played in Freedom Summer and in the civil rights movement as a whole. Why has this role remained largely hidden from view?

WOMANPOWER UNLIMITED came into being as a Movement for Social Action among Women May 29, 1961 in Jackson, Mississippi, concomitant with the arrival of the Freedom Riders on May 26. In the course of its activity more than 200 women, White and Negro, have participated directly in its program. . . .

Clarie Collins Harvey Papers, 1907–1999, Amistad Research Center, Tulane University, New Orleans, La., box 63, folder 12.

The Statement of Purpose

WE, the women of the state of Mississippi, are organizing Woman-power Unlimited in Mississippi communities. Through it, we propose to help create the atmosphere, the institutions, and traditions that make freedom and peace possible. We are all women working together for a peaceful world and wholesome community life. Mississippi must be a better place to live and work because of our efforts.

We mean by freedom:

- the right to speak and organize, to think and write, to work and play, to register to vote as we choose without intervention from those who would keep us silent slaves; the right to be different from the crowd; the right to walk alone and unafraid with God guiding our path;

- the right to initiate and participate in peaceful protests and petitions of grievance against arbitrary and unjust laws; the right to support, in whatever way we can, those others who protest also; for the right to oppose an unconstitutional law is deep in our moral and legal tradition;

- the right to coordinate our activities with and to be a part of peace movements, such as WOMEN STRIKE FOR PEACE, which protests nuclear testing and the arms race and works to achieve general and complete disarmament,

- FOR we believe that the quest for peace and the survival of mankind is the highest form of patriotism.

Where there are no movements or organized efforts to bring about such freedoms, we shall take the initiative. Where efforts in these directions exist, we shall attempt to stimulate more creative and effective action and to cooperate in achieving abundant life for all of us by lending our "womanpower."

We are a movement—without membership, without dues—open to all women who wish to develop their leadership abilities and to make a significant contribution to the good life beyond their homes, local churches, and club groups. . . .

Activities—1961–1964

The activities of Womanpower have included services to the Freedom Riders; participation in registration and voting activities under a grant from the Voter Education Project of the Southern Regional Council . . . ; Prayer Fellowship (interracial) cooperatively with representatives of United Church Women and the Prayer Band of Pearl Street AME Church; Education for Peace Activities; participation with Women Strike For Peace in Peace Pilgrimages to the 17 Nation Disarmament Conferences in Geneva, Switzerland, 1962 and to Rome, Italy in 1963 for an audience with Pope John XXIII in support of his . . . tremendous contributions to world peace and brotherhood; serving as an observer for Women Strike for Peace and Womanpower Unlimited at the "World Without the Bomb Peace Conference," Accra, Ghana, June 1962; attempting to keep doors open by entering and testing facilities of public accommodation; working closely with the National Association for the Advancement of Colored People in a Selective Buying Campaign, May 1963–May 1964; and other activities of similar nature.

Activities of Womanpower with the 1964 Mississippi Summer Project

I The nature of these activities has been:

A Interpretative

1 . . . Many COFO workers attended sessions of Womanpower Unlimited at Campbell College . . . and participated in discussion for the purpose of helping us learn something of the nature of the project so that we might know personally some of those responsible for its planning and implementation and that they might know us and further to determine some of the needs that WU might assist in fulfilling. This information was channeled to the community through WU NEWSLETTERS. . . .

B Supportive

1 Freedom Houses

a Completely furnished the Rose Street Freedom House

b Purchased and installed a refrigerator in the COFO offices . . .

c Provided linens, towels, curtains for the Freedom Houses . . .

d Provided breakfast foods, snack items and cooking utensils

    2 Housing

        a Of Summer Project participants in our homes and in the homes secured by us of friends and acquaintances . . .

II Direct Participation

  A Food

     1 Hot meals were served to the project workers at the COFO office during June and July

     2 In July, . . . a Jackson community Food Project was begun and . . . WU, church and club ladies served hot meals at the church seven (7) days a week—2 to 4 pm on weekdays and 1 to 3 pm on Sundays. In this air-conditioned comfort, workers are receiving balanced, delicious meals and have a central place where ministers, lawyers, women, students, visitors and others come daily. In three weeks time 1400 meals have been served ranging from 35 to 133 persons per day. . . .

     3 Funds have been sought and received from persons within and without the Jackson community to meet these needs. . . .

     4 Breakfast and snack foods continue to be supplied to the Freedom Houses.

     5 Fresh fruit and snacks are being provided for teachers and students of the Freedom Schools. . . .

  C Freedom Schools

     1 Provided some teachers, transportation for pupils, fresh fruit, clothing, library books and school supplies.

     2 Visited schools and community centers in Meridian, Canton and Hattiesburg.

     3 A special Sunday dinner for all Freedom School teachers in the home of Mrs I S Sanders, August 9, 1964.

  D The Mississippi Freedom Democratic Party—WU ladies participated on each level of this experience. . . .

  F Mississippi Free Theatre

      This group has the support of WU in every way. Tangible evidence of this was a party given at the home of Miss

Dana Johnson for the players by WU ladies and other Jackson friends . . . following the performance of "In White America." . . .

III Special Projects—Invited Guests . . .

2 Quaker ladies from the East came upon the invitation of Womanpower Unlimited to work in the area of communications. They travelled under the Minute of their Friends Fellowship.

The deep concern here was for the white community which is almost entirely excluded from all the marvelous experiences that are occurring in the Negro community. The ladies performed their Ministry of Presence by listening creatively to all segments of the white community from liberals to citizen council members and from the most humble to top members of the power structure and encouraging each to move in whatever manner he or she could in LOVE toward THE BELOVED COMMUNITY. . . .

IV Intimidation, Harassment or Violence on the Part of Private Persons

The only two incidents, to my knowledge, occurred at Shoney's Drive-In in Westland Plaza, Jackson, in July when Mrs Pearl Draine, her family and friends were dining and at the Greyhound Bus Station (Jackson) where Mrs Catchings was slapped while dining. The latter incident has already been reported to the Civil Rights Commission at the Advisory Committee's last session. Mrs Pearl Draine will tell her experiences today. . . .

Summary and Conclusion

It is to be noted that White and Negro women—Jewish, Catholic and Protestant—have shared in the experiences of Womanpower and the Summer Project in seeking to help physically beautiful Mississippi become the glorious place, "the beloved community" that it can become.

A better job might have been done, from our viewpoint of housing, feeding, schools, etc., had COFO in its initial planning and continued programming included some of the Womanpower ladies and other women and men of the community.

Continuing needs seem to be ways to establish all kinds of real communication of truth in the total community, ways of refuting the communist propaganda smear that paralyzes so many and more opportunities for face-to-face creative confrontation among those of divergent viewpoints, development of economic channels and skills to sustain the community. (For example—there are no Manpower Training courses in Mississippi nor have there been for the past eight months.)

Because of these and other continuing needs, we believe that the project should continue. Womanpower Unlimited will be pleased to continue its cooperative relationship with future developments.

3

Community Centers and Freedom Schools

22

JANE STEMBRIDGE, CHARLIE COBB, MENDY SAMSTEIN, AND NOEL DAY

Notes on Teaching in Mississippi

1964

As part of their orientation, freedom school teachers studied this set of instructions, designed to help them understand the purpose of the schools, which were intended to be political as well as "educational." Indeed, teachers were encouraged to use the civil rights movement as a way of making the freedom schools relevant and meaningful. Pedagogy was also important. The document provides specific advice on how to teach, focusing on class discussion rather than rote learning. The key to the freedom schools was the awareness that the students brought with them valuable knowledge and experiences. The classroom, then, was to be a safe place where students were free to ask questions and venture opinions, and the teacher was there to learn as well as teach.

Introduction to the Summer—Jane Stembridge

This is the situation: You will be teaching young people who have lived in Mississippi all their lives. That means that they have been deprived of decent education, from the first grade through high school. It means

"Memorandum to Freedom School Teachers: Overview of the Freedom Schools," Wisconsin Historical Society, Freedom Summer Collection, http://content.wisconsinhistory .org/cdm/compoundobject/collection/p15932coll2/id/42343/show/42298/rec/1.

that they have been denied free expression and free thought. Most of all—it means that they have been denied the right to question.

The purpose of the Freedom Schools is to help them begin to question.

What will they be like? They will all be different—but they will have in common the scars of the system. Some will be cynical. Some will be distrustful. All of them will have a serious lack of preparation both with regard to academic subjects and contemporary issues—but all of them will have knowledge far beyond their years. This knowledge is the knowledge of how to survive in a society that is out to destroy you . . . and the knowledge of the extent of evil in the world. . . .

What will they demand of you? They will demand that you be honest. Honesty is an attitude toward life which is communicated by everything you do. Since you, too, will be in a learning situation—honesty means that you will *ask* questions as well as answer them. It means that if you don't know something you will say so. It means that you will not "act" a part in the attempt to compensate for all they've endured in Mississippi. You can't compensate for that, and they don't want you to try. It would not be *real*, and the greatest contribution that you can make to them is to be real.

Remember this: These young people have been taught by the system not to trust. You have to be trust-*worthy*. It's that simple. Secondly, there is very little if anything that you can teach them about prejudice and segregation. They know. What you can and must do is help them develop ideas and associations and tools with which they can do something *about* segregation and prejudice. . . .

This Is the Situation—Charlie Cobb

. . . Learning here means only learning to stay in your place. Your place is to be satisfied—a "good nigger."

[Students] have learned the learning necessary for immediate survival: that silence is safest, so volunteer nothing; that the teacher is the state, and tell them only what they want to hear; that the law and learning are white man's law and learning.

There is hope and there is dissatisfaction—feebly articulated—both born out of the desperation of needed alternatives not given. This is the generation that has silently made the vow of no more raped mothers—no more castrated fathers; that looks for an alternative to a lifetime of bent, burnt and broken backs, minds, and souls. Where creativity must be molded from the rhythm of a muttered "white son-of-a-bitch"; from the roar of hunger-bloated belly; and from the stench of rain and mud washed shacks.

Problems of Freedom School Teaching—
Mendy Samstein

The Freedom Schools will not operate out of schoolhouses. There will rarely be classrooms, certainty no bells, and blackboards only if they can be scrounged. Freedom Schools in Mississippi will be a low-cost operation since funds will be very limited. . . . As a result, most Freedom Schools will have to be held in church basements, homes, back yards, etc. . . .

In some towns in the state, the students are waiting with great excitement in anticipation of the Freedom Schools. In other areas, however, special interest will have to be created—the teachers themselves will have to recruit students before the Freedom Schools begin. In these places, you will find that you are almost the first civil rights worker to be there, and if you are white, you will almost certainly be the first white civil rights workers to come to the town to stay. You will need to deal with the problem of your novelty as well as with the educational challenge. . . .

The greatest advantage . . . will be the students and, we hope, your approach. In the final analysis, the effectiveness of the Freedom Schools this summer will depend upon the resourcefulness and honesty of the individual teachers—on their ability to relate sympathetically to the students, to discover their needs, and to create an exciting "learning" atmosphere. The informal surroundings, the lack of formal "school" trappings, will probably benefit the creation of this atmosphere more than the shortage of expensive equipment will discourage it. Attendance will not be required, so if the teacher is to have regular attendance from his students, he must offer them a program which continues to attract; this means that he must be a human and interesting person.

It is important to recognize that these communities are in the process of rapid social change and our Freedom School program, along with the rest of the summer activities, will be in the middle of this ferment. The students will be involved in a number of political activities which will be relatively new in Negro communities in Mississippi. They will be encouraging people to register to vote, organizing political rallies, campaigning for Negro candidates for high public offices, and preparing to challenge the Mississippi Democratic Party. These activities will be a large part of the experience which the students will bring to your classes. In most instances, we believe that this will help the Freedom School program and you should capitalize on these experiences by relating them to classroom work. You will need to know something about these experiences, so you will have the opportunity to share them by canvassing, campaigning, distributing leaflets, etc., with the students. You will define your role more precisely when you arrive by consulting with COFO voter registration people in the area. It will probably be important to the students that you show willingness to work with them but you will have to balance this against your own need to prepare for classes, recreation and tutoring.

In some communities, however, the situation may go beyond this. The community may embark upon more direct kinds of protest, resulting in mass demonstrations, jail, and any number of eventualities. We have no specific suggestions to make if this situation arises. You will have to play it by ear. We can only say that if you are teaching in a Freedom School in Mississippi, you *must* keep a sensitive ear to the ground so that if this should happen, you will be aware of what is happening in the community. . . .

Remarks to the Freedom School Teachers about Method—Noel Day

TEACHING TECHNIQUES AND METHOD

The curriculum is flexible enough to provide for the use of a wide range of methods in transmitting the material. The basic suggested method is discussion (both as a class and in small groups) because of the opportunities this method provides for:

1. Encouraging expression.
2. Exposing feelings (bringing them into the open where they may be dealt with productively).
3. Permitting the participation of students on various levels.
4. Developing group loyalties and responsibility.
5. Permitting the sharing of strengths and weaknesses of individual group members.

However, presentation lectures, reading aloud (by students), the use of drama, art, and singing can be utilized in many sections of the curriculum. We recommend, however, that discussion be used as a follow up in each instance in order to make certain that the material has been learned.

TEACHING HINTS

1. Material should be related whenever possible to the experience of students.

2. No expression of feelings (hostility, aggression, submission, etc.) should ever be passed over, no matter how uncomfortable the subject or the situation is. Both the students and the teacher can learn something about themselves and each other if it is dealt with honestly and with compassion.

3. The classroom atmosphere should not be formal (it is not a public school). Ways of accomplishing an informal atmosphere might be arrangement of seats in a circle, discussions with individuals or small groups before and after sessions, use of first names between teachers and students, shared field-work experiences, letting students lead occasionally, etc. . . .

8. At the beginning of each session, summarize the material that was covered the day before (or ask a student to do it). . . .

10. Don't be too critical at first; hold criticism until a sound rapport has been established. Praise accomplishments wherever possible. . . .

USING DRAMA

Probably the best way of using the dramatic method is the extemporaneous approach. In this approach, learning lines in a formal way is avoided. A story is told, or a "let us suppose that" or a "Pretend that . . ." situation is structured, and then parts assigned. The actors are encouraged to use their own language to interpret the story or situation and some participants are assigned to act the part of nonhuman objects as well (e.g., trees, a table, a mirror, the wind, the sun, etc.). Each actor is asked to demonstrate how he thinks the character he is portraying looks, what expression, what kind of voice, how he walks, what body posture, etc. As soon as each actor has determined the characteristics of his part, the story outlined is reviewed again, and then dramatized.

23

JOYCE BROWN

The House of Liberty
1964

In McComb, the Ku Klux Klan had bombed the house that was to be used for the freedom school. When the school opened in mid-July, classes were held in the backyard of the bombed building because no black institution dared offer its facilities. Joyce Brown, a sixteen-year-old student, addressed the problem in the following poem. Impressed—and shamed—by her poem, local people soon made church facilities available for the freedom school. In early August, ten black businessmen met secretly. Joyce Brown's poem was read, and the men were so moved that they formed a housing committee and a food committee to assist the COFO staff, and each man contributed fifty dollars toward the purchase of a lot on which to build a community center.

I come not for fortune, nor for fame,
I seek not to add glory to an unknown name,
I did not come under the shadow of night,
I came by day to fight for what's right,
I shan't let fear, my monstrous foe,
Conquer my soul with threat and woe,
Here I have come and here I will stay,
And no amount of fear my determination can sway.

I asked for your churches, and you turned me down,
But I'll do my work if I have to do it on the ground,
You will not speak for fear of being heard,
So you crawl in your shell and say, "Do not disturb,"
You think because you've turned me away,
You've protected yourself for another day.

But tomorrow surely will come,
And your enemy will still be there with the rising sun,

Joyce Brown, "The House of Liberty," 1964, Civil Rights Movement Veterans, www .crmvet.org/poetry/pbrown.htm.

He'll be there tomorrow as all tomorrows in the past,
And he'll follow you into the future if you let him pass.

You've turned me down to humor him,
Ah! Your fate is sad and grim,
For even though your help I ask,
Even without it, I'll finish my task.

In a bombed house I have to teach school
Because I believe all men should live by the Golden Rule.
To a bombed house your children must come,
Because of your fear of a bomb.

And because you've let your fear conquer your soul,
In this bombed house these minds I must try to mold.
I must try to teach them to stand tall and be a man,
When you their parents have cowered down and refused to take a
    stand.

24

LIZ FUSCO

Freedom Schools in Mississippi
1964

In this report, COFO staff member Liz Fusco explains how the freedom schools transformed both the students and the teachers. The schools empowered young blacks to critically examine the world around them and to develop solutions to problems facing them and their families. The teachers encouraged participants to see themselves as actors in the world, capable of challenging authority and making changes in their communities and in the nation.

Although the freedom schools in Mississippi had ceased operation by the spring of 1965, their legacy has endured. Mississippi's head start program, the Child Development Group of Mississippi (CDGM), adopted the pedagogical principles of the freedom schools and had direct ties to

CORE Papers, reel 45, frames 201–4.

the movement. More recently, the Children's Defense Fund initiated a national freedom school program, serving more than nine thousand students at 130 sites. And in Sunflower County, a freedom school has been in operation since the 1990s.

The decision to have Freedom School in Mississippi . . . seems to have been a decision to enter into every phase of the lives of the people of Mississippi. It seems to have been a decision to set the people free for politics in the only way that people really can become free, and that is totally. . . .

It was the asking of questions . . . that made the Mississippi Summer Project different from other voter registration projects and other civil rights activities everywhere else in the South. And so it is reasonable that the transformations that occurred—and transformations that did not occur—out of the Freedom School experience occurred because for the first time in their lives kids were asking questions.

The way the curriculum finally came out was that it was based on the asking of certain questions, questions which kept being asked through the summer. . . . The so-called "Citizenship Curriculum" set up two sets of questions. The primary set was 1. why are we (teachers and students) in Freedom Schools? 2. what is the Freedom Movement? 3. what alternatives does the Freedom Movement offer us? What was called the secondary set of questions, but what seemed to me the more important, because more personal, set was: 1. what does the majority culture have that we want? 2. what does the majority culture have that we don't want? 3. what do we have that we want to keep?

The answering of these questions, and the continual raising of them in many contexts, may be said perhaps to be what the Freedom Schools were about. This was so because in order to answer anything out of what these questions suggest, it is necessary for the student to confront the question of who he is, and what his world is like, and how he fits into it or is alienated from it. . . .

The . . . kids began to see two things at once: that the North was no real escape, and that the South was not some vague white monster doomed irrationally to crush them. Simultaneously, they began to discover that they themselves could take action against the injustices—the specific injustices and the condition of injustice—which kept them unhappy and impotent.

Through the study of Negro History they began to have a sense of themselves as a people who could produce heroes. . . . How is Bob Moses like Moses in the Bible? How is he different? Why did Harriet

Tubman go back into the South after she had gotten herself free in the North—and why so many times? And why doesn't Mrs. Hamer stay in the North once she gets there to speak, since she doesn't have a job on that man's plantation any more, and since her life is in so much danger? . . . And why are the changes of gospel songs into Freedom songs significant? What does "We Shall Overcome" really mean in terms of what we are doing, and what we can do? . . .

Within the Freedom Schools, especially by comparing the Freedom Schools with the regular schools, they began to become articulate about what was wrong, and the way things should be instead: why don't they do this at our school? was the first question asked, and then there began to be answers, which led to further questions, such as why don't our teachers register to vote, if they presume to teach us about citizenship? and why can't our principal make his own decisions instead of having to follow the orders of the white superintendent? and why do we have no student government, or why doesn't the administration take the existing student government seriously?

This was the main question, which came also out of why there are no art classes, no language classes, why there is no equipment in the science labs, why the library is inadequate and inaccessible, why the classes are overcrowded. The main question was WHY ARE WE NOT TAKEN SERIOUSLY? which is of course the question that the adults were asking about the city and county and state, and the question the Freedom Democratic Party asked—and for which the Party demanded an answer—at the Convention. . . .

The transformation of Mississippi is possible because the transformation of people has begun. And if it can happen in Mississippi, it can happen all over the South. The original hope of the Freedom School plan was that there would be about 1000 students in the state coming to the informal discussion groups and other sessions. It turned out that by the end of the summer the number was closer to 3000, and that the original age expectation of 16-17-18 year olds had to be revised to include pre-school children and all the way up to 70 year old people, all anxious to learn about how to be Free. The subjects ranged from the originally anticipated Negro History, Mississippi Now, and black-white relations to including typing, foreign languages, and other forms of tutoring. . . .

To think of the kids in Mississippi expressing emotion on paper with crayons and in abstract shapes rather than taking knives to each other; to think of them writing and performing plays about the Negro experience in America rather than just sitting in despairing lethargy within that experience; to think of their organizing and running all by themselves a Mississippi Student Union, whose program is not dances and fund-raising but direct action to alleviate serious grievances; to think, even, of their being willing to come to school *after school*, day after day, when their whole association with school had been at least uncomfortable and dull and at the worst tragically crippling—to think of these things is to think that a total transformation of the young people in an underdeveloped country can take place, and to dare to dream that it can happen all over the South.

25

THE STUDENT VOICE

Mississippi Harassment

July 15, 1964

The Wide Area Telephone Service (WATS), initiated by the Bell system in 1961, was a flat-rate long-distance service between a central office phone and other phone stations within a specific geographical area. COFO initiated its WATS system in 1964 so that the central office in Jackson could keep track of what was going on in projects across the state. The selections below, taken from phoned-in reports early in the summer and printed in the SNCC newspaper, The Student Voice, *present a picture of harassment and violence directed against civil rights workers by both white civilians and police officers. This list represents a tiny sample of many hundreds of such reports.*

Clinton, June 26—The Church of the Holy Ghost was damaged by fire in the fifth firebombing in ten days in Mississippi.

Jackson, June 27—A white CORE worker, jailed for three weeks along with seven other rights workers, was beaten by white prisoners in the Hinds County jail.

Ruleville, June 28—The mayor of Ruleville prevented a white Stanford University chaplain from attending services at a white church here.

SNCC Papers, reel 73, frame 121.

Jackson, June 28—A summer volunteer was kicked from behind by a local white youth at the train station here as he arrived from Oxford, Ohio.

Hattiesburg, June 29—Two cars belonging to SNCC volunteers were shot at outside the SNCC office here. . . .

Biloxi, June 29—Several white volunteers working in SNCC's pilot white community project were turned away from two hotels here.

Holly Springs, June 30—A white man assaulted SNCC worker Larry Rubin and threatened to "shoot up" the SNCC office.

Harmony (Carthage), June 30—The (white) county superintendent of schools suddenly announced a special session for Negroes only, two days prior to the scheduled opening of a Freedom School here.

Harmony, July 2—Local citizens were told they could not use the Freedom School by the sheriff and county school superintendent. A cross was burned and six pounds of large roofing tacks were spread across roads of the Negro community.

Meridian, July 3—The 11-year-old brother of missing rights worker James Chaney received a broken arm when a white man's car ran a red light forcing the cars to collide.

Hattiesburg, July 3—A Negro grocery store and teen spot was hit by dynamite. . . .

Clarksdale, July 3—A store manager told his Negro employees they would be "discharged" if they went to the courthouse.

Batesville, July 3—A Negro man was struck by a white man as he left the Panola County courthouse.

Laurel, July 4—Two brothers, part of a group of seven Negro teenagers who attempted to test the public accommodations provisions of the civil rights law, were wounded by a mob of 25–30 whites.

Batesville, July 4—A local citizen and summer volunteer were chased in their car for thirty miles. . . .

Jackson, July 5—A white car hurled bottles at the project office here cutting a local woman's leg.

Clarksdale, July 5—Two white volunteers were denied entrance to the (white) First Christian Church.

Jackson, July 6—A local Negro was told he faced $311 in fines and three months in jail on unspecified charges after he was visited by a summer volunteer. . . .

Gulfport, July 7—The tires of a summer worker's car were slashed after she drove local citizens to the courthouse to register to vote.

Vicksburg, July 7—White youths threw a bottle, breaking a window, at a car waiting to pick up Freedom School students.

Moss Point, July 7—Three Negroes, but no whites, were arrested here when they followed a car of whites believed to have shot into a mass meeting here. The shots had injured a 17-year-old girl who was hospitalized for stomach wounds. . . .

Hattiesburg, July 8—The Rev. Robert Beech of the National Council of Churches was arrested on a false pretenses charge for allegedly overdrawing his local bank account. Bond was set at $2,000.

McComb, July 8—A SNCC worker and summer volunteer were injured when the SNCC Freedom House was bombed. The house contained ten project workers, six of them SNCC staff. . . .

McComb, July 9—A car with four white males is reported to have fired on the only Negro on the McComb police force following a SNCC mass meeting.

Gulfport, July 9—Three SNCC summer volunteers were arrested in front of the Harrison County courthouse as they accompanied local citizens to the voting registrar's office.

Greenwood, July 10—Phil Moore, a SNCC volunteer, reported he was beaten and hit with a club by a representative of the Interstate Insurance Company who told him to "get out of town."

Hattiesburg, July 10—Three summer volunteers were assaulted by two white youths with metal bars and beaten on their way to SNCC canvassing headquarters. All three, including a rabbi, were released after hospital treatment.

Greenwood, July 10—SNCC worker Fred Mangrum was singled out of a group of 12 SNCC workers and arrested for profanity. . . .

Jackson, July 10—FBI director J. Edgar Hoover told newsmen the FBI would give "no protection" to civil rights workers.

26

ELLEN LAKE AND BOB

Letters Home from Summer Volunteers

1964

Among the most arresting and revealing documents from Freedom Summer are the letters from volunteers to family and friends back home. At the end of the summer, more than a hundred volunteers decided that they wanted to remain in Mississippi. This was a development the COFO planners had not anticipated: They had assumed that all the volunteers would return home at the end of the summer project. In these two letters, Ellen explains to her parents why she wants to stay in the state and continue to work in black communities, and Bob focuses on the day-to-day work of voter registration and political organizing and the immense challenges faced by black people in Mississippi. In what ways did the experience of volunteering in Mississippi change the authors of these letters? What can be learned about Freedom Summer from reading these letters that is less visible in the more formal documents written by COFO staff members and other veteran activists?

Ellen

Dear Mother and Father,

I have thought a great deal about your letter and my own feelings. I've been mulling over your arguments and my ideas—and they are finally coming together in this letter.

It seems to me that you have broken down the question of my staying in Mississippi into two separate questions: whether I should work with COFO in Mississippi, and whether I should work here during the year to come.

Concerning the first, you talk about my skills being better utilized in another sphere, another world. While it is true that a SNCC worker who grew up in Gulfport would be better able than I to talk to his neighbors,

Compiled from Ellen Lake Papers, 1964, Archives Main Stacks, SC 3057, State Historical Society of Wisconsin, Madison, Wis., folder 1; and William Heath Papers, box 3, folder 1.

I think you are closing your eyes to the ways in which my skills are useful here.

Foremost is the consideration that working in Gulfport—or in any Mississippi town—is not primarily a problem of working with Negroes, but of working with people. What we are trying to do down here is to make both Negroes and whites understand that they are people first and black or white second, and that they deserve the rights and treatment of people.

We do this by treating them as people. This I can do—rather well, I'm finding out. . . . I've been able to reach these people, to communicate with them, to make them see themselves and others in a new light.

. . . Take Bettie Drummond, a young woman just 21 years old and one of my closest friends here. One of the other COFO workers said that when he first contacted her, she wouldn't sign a Freedom Form and showed no interest in registering. After I talked to her, she went down to the courthouse and is now a block captain and one of the sharpest in the group. Last week I organized a meeting of block captains in North Gulfport—all people whom I have gotten involved in the Movement—and now they are planning a bus boycott. They couldn't have done this two months ago.

You speak of losing focus from spending a year in Mississippi; but what kind of focus do I have? All of my nineteen years I have shuttled between Westchester, Martha's Vineyard, the Virgin Islands, summer camp and Radcliffe—how can I help but gain a new perspective from Mississippi? For the first time in my life, I am seeing what it is like to be poor, oppressed, and hated. And what I see here does not apply only to Gulfport or to Mississippi or even to the South. It is the plight of perhaps a billion people throughout the world.

This summer puts a great deal more in focus. Don expressed it beautifully when he was telling me about interviewing people on the streets of Winston-Salem, after the President's Viet Nam speech. Most of the passers said something about "dropping a couple of bombs on the dirty bastards and showing them who is boss." The only people who saw things in focus were the four Negroes whom he interviewed. They all said, "Maybe the President is right, but the whole thing is awfully confused, and what are we shooting and bombing people on the other side of the world for when we have so many of our own problems here in Mississippi and Harlem?"

The people we're killing in Viet Nam are the same people whom we've been killing for years in Mississippi. True, we didn't tie the knot in Mississippi and we didn't pull the trigger in Viet Nam—that is, we personally—but we've been standing behind the knot-tiers and the trigger-pullers too long. We've got a hell of a lot to atone for, and not much time to do it in. . . .

Your command that I return home after the summer was entirely divorced from my reasons and ideas. It was an arbitrary order based on your own wishes and what you thought my ideas might be. But because you had not spent the summer in Mississippi, you could not really understand my reasons, any more than I could have explained them to you three months ago. . . . My decision to come to Mississippi this summer could not be based on any real knowledge of what awaited me here; inevitably it had to be colored by the excitement of a dangerous adventure, by the glamour of being able to say casually, "Oh, I'm going to Mississippi for summer," and take in people's gasps of surprise.

But I have been here nearly two months. I know the drudgery, the dangers, and the disappointments. I know what it's like to eat meatless dinners, to be so exhausted you feel as though you will drop, to have five people show up at a meeting to which 20 should have come. Yet I also know what it's like to sing, "We Shall Overcome" with 200 others till you think the roof will explode off the church. I know what it's like to see the organization which you have nurtured come to life and begin to function and create. I know what it's like to have a choir of little girls sing out, "Hi, Ellen," as I walk down the road and envelop me in their hugs.

Only now that I know these things can the decision to stay be mature and meaningful.

Furthermore, maturity does not develop from facing a familiar routine. . . . Maturity comes from having to face new situations, from making new decisions, from coming to terms with a new world. The same is true of education: it comes not so much from an evening at Radcliffe Library as from two hours of talking to a Mississippi Negro who is in tears about the degradation of having to go to the other side of the bus station to buy a ticket. I have learned more about politics from running my own precinct meetings than I could have from any Gov professor. And I'm sure that I will appreciate more the academic education which I will resume after the practical one I get here.

About the things which have to be done in the North, they will be there for a long time—a lot longer than I will be around to do them. I'm going to spend the rest of my life being a white liberal; let me have one year to see what lies below that veneer. . . .

This summer is only the briefest beginning of this experience—both for myself and for the Negroes of Mississippi. So much of it will seem pointless if it ends now, or if it is taken up again in two years. A war cannot be fought and won if the soldiers take twelve-month leaves after every skirmish.

For these reasons, I ask that you reconsider your refusal to allow me to spend the coming year in Mississippi. If you consent, I will spend the month of September at home, raising money and support among local friends and acquaintances and would probably head back around the beginning of October. Such fund-raising/vacation intervals would be taken throughout the year.

Think about what I have written. You were once before able to throw over the natural sentiment of "I know it has to be done, but does it have to be you?" It still must be done—and I would like it to be me.

Your daughter,

Ellen

P.S. I have considered your parental qualms; really I have. But I'm afraid they cannot counterbalance the feelings of my duty here.

Bob

Dear Dad

Please excuse the carbon; I have not much time.

I want to tell you about Mississippi and about the Freedom Movement here. It is not easy; my impressions are many and very strong. I have met the best and worst people here, the greatest courage and the greatest terror—sometimes in the same person. This Mississippi is a beautiful land of red earth and a thousand greens, made ugly by the squalor and hate which dominate the races who live here.

I work in voter registration. Three of us work together; one is a Negro. In as many cases as possible the Negro is made the project director, and such is the case here. The policy is a wise and effective one. On a normal day we roll out of bed early in the morning. We may have slept in the Freedom House, or in the home of some generous and brave farmer (two essential requirements for anyone to offer us hospitality). We study the map of the county, decide where we will work for the day. We scramble for breakfast and hit the road.

The work is long and hot. We drive from farmhouse to farmhouse. I have averaged almost 200 miles a day on the car. The roads are in despicable condition. We know where the colored people are by those roads:

where the pavement stops the Negro sections are likely to begin. And if there is not even gravel on the roads, we can be reasonably sure that we are in a "safe" neighborhood. Such is not always the case, though, and more than once we have been cursed and threatened by someone for knocking on a white man's door.

When we walk up to a house there are always children out front. They look up and see white men in the car, and fear and caution cover their expressions. Those terrified eyes are never quite out of my mind; they drive me as little else could. Children who have hardly learned to talk are well-taught in the arts of avoiding whites. They learn "yassah" as almost their first words. If they did not, they could not survive. The children run to their parents, hide behind them. We walk up, smile, say howdy, and hold out our hands. "As we shake hands I tell them my name. They tell me their names and I say Mr. ____, how do you do. It is likely the first time in the life of this farmer or housewife a white man has ever shaken hands with them, or even called them "with a handle to their names." This does not necessarily bode well to them; they are suspicious. Chances are they have heard about the "freedom riders" passing through. The news is usually greeted with mingled fear, excitement, enthusiasm and gratitude. But the confrontation is more serious and more threatening. They think, if Mr. Charlie knew . . . , and they are afraid. They have good reason to be. Murders of Negroes in Mississippi are not news. No one cares, and no one is surprised. Much as teenagers in our northern cities cruise the streets and whistle at girls, white teenagers down here abuse Negroes. They go night-riding five in a car, and woe to him caught alone on the road. They throw bottles at homes and people; they even shoot into cars. There is not a lawman in the state who would arrest them for such an activity. Young girls never go out alone at night. All this appears before them as we speak, and it is this they fear. Many, too, are share-croppers, who must turn over a third to a half of the year's harvest to a man who does no work at all, but who owns the land they till. They may be evicted, and have often been for far less serious offenses. Nearly everyone black in Mississippi is at least a year in debt. The threat of suspended credit and foreclosure is a tremendous burden; our presence adds much to the load. A wage for a laborer is usually $2.50 to $3 a day for work from six to six. There is no job security, no sick benefit (often if you get sick you get fired), no old age pensions. Very often Negroes know nothing about welfare or social security. They have no insurance against misfortune.

Yet they listen when we speak. We tell them we are from the North. We tell them that the nation has finally become interested in them, and concerned over their plight. We talk about taxes, and cotton allotments, and usury, and schools and hospitals and federal agencies. We talk about dignity. People listen, and they wonder. They are not sure. What does it mean when a white man tells them the truth, when he asks them to help him, to help themselves? Why is he here? What does he really want? What will come of it? We tell them about the Freedom Democratic Party, about the Convention Challenge in Atlantic City. We talk about a Negro sheriff and blacktop roads and respect. They listen and they wonder. They think of their children, of the danger, of the odds. And more often than not, they sign up for the Freedom Democratic Party.

This new party in this state is going to be the salvation of the black man and of the white. There is not the bitterness here that there is in Chicago, in Harlem. People in the North have tried and failed. Here they are trying for the first time.

Twice in the last five days we have held precinct and county meetings, in DeSoto and Tippah counties. DeSoto is very poor, and 62% Negro. Tippah is surprisingly wealthy and about 20% Negro. The meetings attracted about 110 people in DeSoto and about 40 people in Tippah (after only three days' work).

Our job is a seven-day, fifteen-hour job, except when there are mass meetings (at least twice a week), when it is longer. We have extensive reports to write up (in quadruplicate; we need a ditto reproducing machine badly), staff meetings, strategy planning. It is the most stimulating, satisfying work I have ever done. Nothing is ever enough; there is no such thing as a job finished: there is only progress. We are involved here in a process of uniting, joining, becoming a mutually interested community. The song says it well: we shall overcome.

Yours,

/s/ Bob

4

Demanding the Right to Vote

27

BOB MOSES

Emergency Memorandum
July 19, 1964

*In this document, Bob Moses sent out a clarion call to the COFO staff
and volunteers to step up the process of registering people for the Mississippi Freedom Democratic Party. After several years of focusing on add-
ing black names to the state's voter registration rolls, Moses asked the staff
to focus on the parallel registration for the MFDP. Recognizing that the
culmination of the summer project was the convention challenge, Moses
understood that its success depended on the complex process of following
state election law. This required plenty of labor from a limited staff. One
month into Freedom Summer, the focus of the organizers shifted to the
political challenge. Why do you think the organization for the MFDP was
behind schedule?*

The various political programs which [comprise] the Freedom Democratic Party's Convention Challenge are in very bad shape all around the
state. A further problem that the FDP coordinators have found is that in
general, the staff around the state are either unconvinced of the importance of the convention challenge to COFO's work, or are not aware of
the massive job which remains to be done in order to be prepared for
the challenge. If we are to have any degree of success, everyone who

SNCC Papers, reel 40, frames 62–65.

is not working in Freedom Schools or community centers must devote all their time to organizing for the convention challenge. Some staff members have very honestly admitted that they were unaware of the urgency of the situation and therefore didn't realize that the Challenge should be given priority until mid-August. It is the feeling of the FDP coordinators that in part the misunderstanding is the fault of the Project and Program Directors, who did not properly stress the importance of the programs. At any rate, all of us must now pull together behind the program in order to make it at least a partial success. . . .

Develop what seem to be weak areas: counties around Columbus, some of the Fourth District counties, and the Northern Second District. In these areas meetings should be held if at all possible. This doesn't mean a big meeting necessarily, but a small one in someone's home maybe. These meetings should select delegates to District and State Conventions, even if it means that all the people at the meeting come as delegates. The important thing may be to draw people into a statewide organization that can support them in some way as we continue to organize those areas. Don't give up because you can't pull a big meeting off. Round up a few people for a meeting or if necessary just bring them to the District or State Convention. . . .

The Need for Reevaluation of Freedom Days and National Voter Registration Techniques in View of the Present Circumstances

The staff is supposedly agreed as to the value of organizing the Freedom Democratic Party and challenging the delegation of the Mississippi Democratic Party to the Democratic National Convention, as opposed to expending all of our manpower to the end that inconsequential numbers of Negroes become officially registered. In view of this fact it is our feeling that—

1. *Freedom Days* which require the energies of the staff to organize and execute, and in which they might be arrested, *should not be held.* This is because they are not directly geared to getting people Freedom Registered and therefore the arrest of key staff in this activity cannot even be used as an argument for the seating of our delegation. Mass arrests during Freedom Registration Days are *good grounds for challenge.* They present a reason as to why we were not able to get 425,000 people on the Freedom Registration books.

2. Time should not be spent taking people down to the court-house—*unless* they *ask* to be taken down. After August 20th or so we will have ample opportunity to try to convince people to register—*if* we feel that the psychological value of getting a few people "to try" is worthwhile. We *cannot* do everything at one time and the Challenge, which we have committed ourselves to, is *by itself* an overwhelming task for our limited staff.

3. We do have time to partially rectify the Freedom Registration situation, but the Precinct organization must be done *immediately* and *if it is done correctly there will be no time to do regular voter registration work.*

4. The FDP is *not* a "special interest group"; the VR volunteers (upwards of 400 people) should be working full time. All staff members and VR volunteers are FDP organizers and are responsible for the status of the party's organization.

28

MISSISSIPPI STATE SOVEREIGNTY COMMISSION

Report on Civil Rights Activity

January–August 1964

The white opposition to the civil rights movement in Mississippi was diverse. Members of the Citizens' Council, formed in 1954 to oppose school desegregation, were often prominent business and professional men, along with elected officials. The Council worked closely with the Mississippi State Sovereignty Commission, established as a spy and propaganda agency by the Mississippi legislature in the aftermath of the Brown *decision. This report records some of the activities the commission and its agents engaged in preceding and during Freedom Summer. The list represents a tiny sample of many hundreds of such actions designed to thwart movement*

Mississippi State Sovereignty Commission, http://mdah.state.ms.us/arrec/digital _archives/sovcom/.

activity. Neither the Citizens' Council nor the Sovereignty Commission
succeeded in destroying the movement in Mississippi.

In January, the three investigators were assigned to make personal contacts with new sheriffs about the work of the Sovereignty Commission and to suggest mutual cooperation and exchange of information. The investigators also, during these trips, updated the county files on activities of racial agitators. We wrote a digest of various laws the sheriffs could use in dealing with agitators and made other suggestions as to how the sheriffs could best deal with the outside students when they came to Mississippi this summer. . . .

In February, we had consultations with WLBT and General Motors dealers to determine if "Bonanza" could be dropped by WLBT after three Bonanza stars refused to appear as scheduled for a public appearance in Jackson. They gave as their reasons they would not perform before a segregated audience. WLBT was unable to justify cancellation of this program. . . .

We advised the management of Jackson City Lines about a planned attempt to boycott city busses. We also advised Jackson City Lines of the names of the leaders who were planning the project. The boycott eventually played out as the leaders were unable to provide suitable transportation as a substitute. . . .

The Investigation Department in June began a detailed investigation of Rust College at Holly Springs which had become a headquarters for COFO workers. Information very detrimental to the President of the college and other activities of the school have been compiled and presented to members of the Board of Trustees for possible action. The trustees have been impressed with these reports which involve communistic activities at the college as well as racial agitation. No action had been taken at the time this report was written. . . .

On June 24, 1964, the Sovereignty Commission had a visit from Allen Dulles who had been sent to Mississippi by President Johnson for a personal look at Mississippi's situation. We had prepared a memorandum especially for Mr. Dulles on Mississippi in general and we showed him documents that linked communist front organizations with racial agitators. Mr. Dulles asked for additional reports on communist activities in the state. A 16 page memorandum was prepared and sent to the Governor's office.

There are many cases where proprietors operating public accommodations businesses are calling on the Sovereignty Commission for guidance. We have recommended that they not comply with the civil rights bill and we have furnished them with information as to steps being taken by others in the same predicament. . . .

Council of Federated Organizations

Through various informers and sources, we have kept up to date with all the plans of the Council of Federated Organizations, who invaded Mississippi and set up freedom schools and voter registration centers. We have many names of students on file as well as lawyers from the National Lawyers Guild, a communist front organization, who have been in Mississippi to assist civil rights workers. Many of these students were found to have communist backgrounds. We worked with Mayor W. O. Williford in Drew in setting up a trial court to make information available to the press about some of these students and attorneys. We wrote to each sheriff in the state and asked that they furnish us with the names, addresses, and any other information they might have on COFO workers in their county so that we might check them for any communist associations. We will advise the sheriffs if we discover the COFO workers are affiliated with communists. . . .

Canton Boycott

Since January 1964, the Commission has been working with the merchants in Canton attempting to adopt a program that would reduce effectiveness of a Negro boycott against Canton merchants. We have made several recommendations. . . .

Negro Applications in Colleges and Universities

Several Negroes have applied for admission in various state supported educational institutions. The College Board refers these applications to our department and we conduct investigations. Several have been discouraged and others are still pending.

"Oxford, U.S.A."

The film "Oxford, U.S.A." has been distributed to many audiences in many states. It has appeared before groups in Massachusetts (four showings), New Hampshire, Iowa, New York, California, Ohio, Indiana, and Montana, since January 1, 1964. . . .

Mississippi Freedom Democratic Party

The Sovereignty Commission has kept close tabs on the organizers and participants in the Mississippi Freedom Democratic Party. Some of those who have been behind the movement are indexed in our subversive file. At the request of the Attorney General's office, we prepared a brief on the Freedom Democratic Party showing that it was organized by non-residents of Mississippi, that its delegation to the national convention in Atlantic City was elected by delegates from only 40 of the 82 counties, and that its membership was composed of individuals associated with communist front organizations. Our material was made part of the brief that accompanied the delegation of regular Mississippi Democrats to Atlantic City.

Philadelphia Case

From the beginning of the Philadelphia case involving three civil rights workers, the Sovereignty Commission had an investigator on the scene. Many extensive reports concerning this case are on file in the Commission office. We have an excellent record of the events that occurred. . . .

Conclusion

In this report we have referred to highlights in activities of the Commission staff during the period from January 1964 to September 1, 1964. Much of the routine work that is carried on by this office has not been mentioned in this report.

29

COUNCIL OF FEDERATED ORGANIZATIONS

Platforms and Principles of the Mississippi Freedom Democratic Party

1964

Founded in early 1964 to give blacks an alternative to the regular white segregated Democratic Party, the MFDP pledged to support the candidates and principles adopted by the national party at its convention in Atlantic City. The platform reveals its commitment to the progressive wing of the Democratic Party on domestic issues, while holding a subtly critical stance on U.S. foreign policy. The Freedom Democrats called for federal action to compel the state of Mississippi to enforce voting rights laws, end segregation in all aspects of public life, and administer various federal antipoverty programs with fairness.

The Freedom Democratic Party, believing that racial equality is only the first step in solving the basic problems of poverty, disease and illiteracy confronting American society, welcomes the participation of all Mississippi citizens in a joint effort to realize the goals of economic growth and individual self-fulfillment . . . for . . . every person.

With all humility we ask the guidance of Almighty God in these difficult times. . . .

We pledge to support the candidates and principles adopted by the National Democratic Party at its convention in Atlantic City in August, 1964.

National Affairs

BE IT RESOLVED:

1. That we support the 1960 national Democratic Party platform, specifically insofar as the following principles apply to the State of Mississippi.

a. Full employment as a fundamental objective of national policy and the necessity for federal aid to the depressed areas of Mississippi and the rest of the nation.

b. Strong state and national action to eliminate artificial barriers to employment based on race, sex, religion, or national origin.

c. The right to a job requires the full restoration of collective bargaining, and the repeal of anti-labor legislation designed to prevent the effective organization of unions.

d. The right of every farmer, tenant, sharecropper and migrant worker to a decent living through the raising of farm incomes and wages, national and state legislation affecting wages and living conditions, food stamp programs to feed needy children, the aged and the unemployed, and the expansion of school lunch and milk programs.

e. Medical care benefits to be provided as part of the Social Security insurance system.

2. That we wholeheartedly endorse the program embodied in the Civil Rights Law of 1964 and that we demand both state and national officials to implement the principles of this law.

3. That we insist that all officials of the state and national governments take steps to ensure the impartial registration of all qualified voters in the State of Mississippi. We urge vigorous enforcement of the civil rights law to guarantee the right to vote to all citizens in all areas of the country. We urge the abolition of the literacy test as a voting requirement. We further urge use of the 14th amendment clause which allows for a reduction in Congressional representation when qualified voters are not registered.

4. That we vigorously support the Supreme Court school desegregation decision of 1954 and demand that immediate measures should be undertaken by the state and national governments to guarantee that the decision be implemented in the State of Mississippi.

5. That we support the Supreme Court re-apportionment decision of 1964 and call for a just system of representation in every legislative body in the United States consistent with the principles that each individual has an equal vote.

6. That we believe that an extensive job re-training program should be vigorously pursued by both the state and national

governments in order that middle-aged people who are victims of an era of economic transition may continue to be self-sufficient members of the community.

7. That we applaud the start which has been made toward the amelioration of poverty under Presidents John F. Kennedy and Lyndon B. Johnson in such measures as area redevelopment, a broadened minimum wage, manpower training, food stamp legislation, and the omnibus anti-poverty measure. We call for the intensification of these programs during the next four years under continued liberal Democratic leadership and for the integration of these efforts with a creative public works program.

8. That we strongly endorse the efforts of Presidents John F. Kennedy and Lyndon B. Johnson to achieve international development and cooperation through such measures as support of the United Nations, vigorous foreign aid programs, attempts to bring about control of nuclear weapons, and the creation of the Peace Corps.

9. That we applaud the advance of freedom throughout the world and advocate American cooperation with the United Nations in a peaceful effort to eradicate tyranny in those areas of the world—such as South Africa, Angola, Southern Rhodesia, Hungary, and East Germany—where it still prevails.

10. That we oppose attempts by any nation or bloc to impose alien political systems or ideologies—communistic or otherwise—on any other nation.

11. That we vigorously condemn extremist and hate groups such as the Ku Klux Klan, the White Citizens' Council, and the Association for the Preservation of the White Race.

Mississippi Affairs

BE IT RESOLVED:

1. That we urge careful consideration of the use of federal funds in Mississippi to ensure that such grants will not be used for the perpetuation of segregation.

   Specifically:

   a. That we oppose the use of federal funds for the construction or maintenance of segregated community facilities in Mississippi.

b. That we advocate the establishment of a state Fair Employment Practices Committee to assist in reviewing cases of employment discrimination.

2. That we advocate careful supervision of the use of federal funds in order that the withholding of federal funds will no longer be used as a means to threaten and harass Mississippi citizens who try to exercise their constitutional rights.

3. That we look for the appointment of federal referees to supervise all Mississippi electoral procedures—from the first attempt to register to vote to the final counting of ballots—until all citizens of the state can rest assured of a meaningful voice in a democratic society.

4. That we advocate a substantial reduction in the state sales tax and a proportionate increase in the income tax.

5. That we condemn the use of state tax monies to support the Sovereignty Commission and other organizations whose aim is to perpetuate the segregated society.

30

ELLA BAKER

Keynote Speech before the State Convention of the Mississippi Freedom Democratic Party
August 6, 1964

Ella Baker was manager of the MFDP's Washington, D.C., office, which became the lobbying arm of the party. Before that, she was the national director of branches for the NAACP and the first executive director of SCLC. She is commonly identified as the founding mother of SNCC. Her keynote speech at the MFDP state convention emphasized the role of the people in defining democracy. She captured the mood of the day in her most memorable line: "Until the killing of black men, black mothers' sons, becomes as

"Ella Baker Speech at the MFDP Convention," ABC News, August 6, 1964, transcribed by Daphne R. Chamberlain. ABC News tape, in the possession of Dr. Chamberlain, courtesy of ABC News.

*important to the rest of the country as the killing of a white mother's son,
we who believe in freedom cannot rest." Baker understood that the safety of
black lives was tied directly to gaining the vote. Why did she believe this?*

To Bob Moses, who truly is a Moses, and at certain stages, a Moses in the wilderness. And to the people who had the mind to listen and respond, you who are here today, I salute you—because it is only as people respond can the work that Bob is attempting or the work that is being attempted to bring freedom to all Americans—it is only as people respond that this is made possible.

I consider this assemblage an assemblage of people who yet have come through the wilderness of fear, who yet have come through the beatings, the harassments, the brutalization that are characteristic not only of Mississippi but unfortunately characteristic of too many areas in America. And I consider this a convention that speaks to the nation and speaks to the world, and its voice is saying that the day has come when racism must be banished from the political body politic of our country and people. . . .

Now, this is not the kind of keynote speech perhaps you like. . . . The South has functioned as an oligarchy. It's made use of its connection . . . with the national or federal government at every point that serves the interest of the South. . . . This is symbolized by the overused phrase, "maintaining the southern way of life." Maintaining the southern way of life meant that the South was outside of the pale of the rest of the life of the country. . . .

It points out the need for political action. It points out how to develop leadership at local levels, and that's why you are here today. You are here because you believe and you know that your life and the lives of all the people of this state have been hamstrung, have been limited, and both white and Negro, if you please, by the very fact that Mr. Eastland and other politicians like Ross Barnett, and even your present governor have subscribed to the theory and practice of racism first and anything else afterwards.

So, what does it add up to? It adds up to the fact that Mississippi has the poorest schools in the whole country. It adds up to the fact that Mississippi is the poorest state in the whole country. It adds up to the fact that hundreds of young people, white and Negro, who scrambled through school somehow—however bad they may be—went away and left the state of Mississippi because there was nowhere for them to work, nothing for them to do. And this is what we speak to.

And those that were dug from the earth only twenty odd miles, I believe, from the scene of where these three people were last seen [James Chaney, Andrew Goodman, and Michael Schwerner]. These three . . . were . . . but a symbol. The unfortunate thing is that it took this kind of symbol to make the rest of the country turn its eyes on the fact that there are other bodies lying under the swamps of Mississippi.

Until the killing of black men, black mothers' sons, becomes as important to the rest of the country as the killing of a white mother's son, we who believe in freedom cannot rest. . . .

What then shall we do? Surely we must do what we are doing now. Surely the Mississippi Freedom Democratic Party will not end after today. The Mississippi Freedom Democratic Party is only beginning, and it is beginning on the basis that it believes that a political party should be open to all the people who wish to subscribe to its principles. That means it's open to even the son of the father on whose plantations you worked if that son has reached the point that he is willing to subscribe to your principles. It means also that the Mississippi Freedom Democratic Party has challenged the power structure of the state of Mississippi at its Achilles heel. As a tender spot, the Achilles heel, the spot you know that kills if you get an arrow right at that spot. And this is why we get the resistance to registration and voting.

31

COUNCIL OF FEDERATED ORGANIZATIONS

List of MFDP Delegates

1964

The MFDP delegation included farmers, sharecroppers, beauticians, teachers, ministers, college students, businesspeople, and three white Mississippians among its ranks. This broad cross section of Mississippians epitomized the cutting edge of the summer project. Most of the names on this list will not be familiar to you. All of the people on this list overcame

Mississippi Freedom Democratic Party Delegation, 1964, Civil Rights Movement Veterans, http://www.crmvet.org/docs/6408_mfdp_delegates.pdf.

fear and risked potential harm to themselves and their families by serving as delegates or alternates. Each person on this list contributed in a significant way to the civil rights movement. Why is it that those who make history are so rarely remembered by historians?

MISSISSIPPI FREEDOM DEMOCRATIC PARTY DELEGATION:

National Committeewoman: Mrs. Victoria Gray
National Committeeman: Rev. Edwin King
Chairman of the delegation: Mr. Aaron Henry
Vice-chairman of the delegation: Mrs. Fannie Lou Hamer
Secretary: Mrs. Annie Devine

DELEGATES:	ALTERNATES:
Mrs. Helen Anderson	Mr. C. R. Darden
Dr. A. D. Beittel	Mrs. Ruby Evans
Mrs. Elizabeth Blackwell	Mr. Oscar Giles
Mrs. Marie Blalock	Mr. Charlie Graves
Mr. Sylvester Bowens	Mrs. Pinkie Hall
Mr. J. W. Brown	Mrs. Macy Hardaway
Mr. Charles Bryant	Mr. Andrew Hawkins
Mr. James Carr	Mr. William Jackson
Miss Lois Chaffee	Mrs. Alta Lloyd
Mr. Chois Collier	Rev. J. F. McRee
Mr. Willie Ervin	Mr. George Harper
Mr. J. C. Fairley	Rev. W. G. Middleton
Mr. Dewey Green	Mr. Joe Newton
Mr. Laurence Guyot	Mrs. M. A. Phelps
Mrs. Winson Hudson	Mrs. Beverly Polk
Mr. Johnny Jackson	Mr. Henry Reaves
Mr. N. L. Kirkland	Mr. Harold Roby
Miss Mary Lane	Mrs. Emma Sanders
Rev. Merrill W. Lindsay	Mrs. Cora Smith
Mrs. Yvonne MacGowen	Rev. R. L. T. Smith
Mr. Eddie Mack	Mrs. Elmira Tyson
Mrs. Lula Matthews	Mr. L. H. Waborn
Mr. Charles McLaurin	
Mr. Leslie McLemore	
Mr. Robert Miles	
Mr. Otis Millsap	

DELEGATES:

Mrs. Hazel Palmer
Rev. R. S. Porter
Mr. Willie Scott
Mr. Henry Sias
Mr. Robert Lee Stinson
Mr. Slate Stallworth
Mr. E. W. Steptoe
Mr. Joseph Stone
Mr. Eddie Thomas
Mr. James Travis
Mr. Hartman Turnbow
Mr. Abraham Washington
Mr. Clifton R. Whitley
Mr. Robert W. Williams
Mr. J. Walter Wright

32

DAVID DENNIS

Eulogy for James Chaney
August 7, 1964

On August 4, 1964, the FBI, acting on a tip from an informant, discovered the bodies of the three murdered civil rights workers in an earthen dam in Neshoba County. Three days later, a memorial service was held for James Chaney. For the first hour, local ministers conducted a low-key service, careful not to inflame the emotions of the audience. When it came his turn to speak, however, COFO leader Dave Dennis looked down at a weeping Ben Chaney, James's little brother, and could not contain his anger. He then delivered one of the most powerful addresses in the movement's short history.

Late in 1967, an all-white Mississippi jury convicted seven men, including Neshoba County Deputy Sheriff Cecil Price and Klan leader

Susie Erenrich, ed., *Freedom Is a Constant Struggle: An Anthology of the Mississippi Civil Rights Movement* (Montgomery, Ala.: Black Belt Press, 1999), 360–63.

Sam Bowers, of the federal crime of violating the rights of the three activists. All defendants were released from prison by the mid-1970s. In 2005, Mississippi journalist Jerry Mitchell's investigative reporting helped lead to the trial and conviction of Edgar Ray Killen, who had orchestrated the Klan killings. Killen had been the beneficiary of a mistrial in 1967 when a single juror voted for his acquittal.

I'm not here to do the traditional thing most of us do at such a gathering. And that is to tell . . . what a great person the individual was. . . . I think we all know because he walked these dusty streets of Meridian . . . before I came here. . . . I don't grieve for Chaney because . . . I feel that he lived a fuller life than many of us will ever live. I feel that he's got his freedom and we are still fighting for it.

But what I want to talk about right now is the living dead that we have right among our midst, not only in the state of Mississippi but throughout the nation. Those are the people who don't care, those who do care but don't have the guts enough to stand up for it, and those people who are busy up in Washington and in other places using my freedom and my life to play politics with. That includes the President on down to the government of the state of Mississippi. . . . In my opinion, as I stand here, I not only blame the people who pulled the trigger or did the beating or dug the hole with the shovel. . . . But I blame the people in Washington D.C. and on down in the state of Mississippi for what happened just as much as I blame those who pulled the trigger. . . .

As I stand here a lot of things pass through my mind. I can remember the Emmett Till case, what happened to him, and what happened to the people who killed him. They're walking the streets right now. . . . I remember . . . the name of Mack Parker and exactly what happened to him and what happened to the people who beat, killed him, and drug him down the streets and threw him in the river. I know that those people were . . . never brought to trial. I can remember . . . in Birmingham . . . the four young kids who were bombed in the church and . . . what has happened to the people who killed them—nothing. Remember the little thirteen year old kid who was riding a bicycle and who was shot in the back? And the youth who shot him, who was a white guy from Birmingham, got off with three months.

I can remember all of that right now. Or I can remember the Medgar Evers case [and Byron De La] Beckwith. The person who was governor of the state at that particular time going up and shaking his hand when the jury said that it could not come to a verdict. I can remember all of that. And I can remember down in the southwest area where you had six Negroes who'd been killed, and I can remember the Lees. . . .

Well I'm getting sick and tired! I'm sick and tired of going to memorials! I'm sick and tired of going to funerals! I've got a bitter vengeance in my heart tonight! And I'm sick and tired and can't help but feel bitter, you see, deep down inside and I'm not going to stand here and ask anybody here not to be angry tonight.

Yeah, we have love in our hearts, and we've had it for years and years in this country. We've died on the battlefield to protect the people in this country . . . , to defend this country and to come back to do what? To live as slaves . . . , and I'm sick and tired of that.

You see, we're all tired. You see, I know what's gonna happen! I feel it deep in my heart! When they find the people who killed these guys in Neshoba County, you've got to come back to the state of Mississippi and have a jury of their cousins, their aunts and their uncles. And I know what they're going to say—not guilty. Because no one saw them pull the trigger. I'm tired of that!

See another thing that makes me even tireder though, and that is the fact that we as people here in this state and the country are allowing this to continue to happen. Even us as black folk. So I look at the young kids here—that's something else that I grieve about. For little Ben Chaney here and the other ones like him around in this audience and around on the streets. I grieve because sometimes they make me feel that, maybe, they have to go through the same thing. . . . And they are gonna have to go through the same thing! Unless we as individuals begin to stand up and demand our rights and a change in this dad-blasted country. . . . We have to stand and demand it because tomorrow, baby, it could be you or your child.

We're going to come to this memorial here, say, "Oh, what a shame," go back home and pray to the Lord as we've done for years. We go back to work in some white folks' kitchen tomorrow, and forget about the whole God-blasted thing, you see.

Don't applaud! Don't applaud! Don't get your frustrations out by clapping your hands. Each and every one of us as individuals is going to have to take it upon ourself to become leaders in our community. Block by block, house by house, city by city, county by county, state by state throughout this entire country. Taking our black brothers by the hand. . . . Holding our hands up high, telling them that if they're not ready for us, "Too bad, baby, 'cause we're coming anyway. . . ."

. . . I watch the people here who go out there and wash dishes and you cook for them. For the whites in the community and those same ones you cook for, wash and iron for, who come right out and say, "I can't sit down and eat beside a nigger," or anything like that. I'm tired of that. . . . I'm tired of him talking about how much he hates me and he can't stand for me to go to school with his children. . . . But yet, when he wants someone to baby-sit for him, he gets my black mammy to hold that baby! And as long as he can do that, he can sit down beside me, he can watch me go up there and register to vote, he can watch me take some type of public office in this state, and he can sit down as I rule over him just as he's ruled over me for years. . . .

This is our country too. We didn't ask to come here when they brought us over here, and I hear the old statement over and over again about me to go back to Africa. Well, I'm ready to go back to Africa, baby, when all the Jews, the Poles, the Russians, the Germans and they all go back to their country where they came from too, you see. And they have to remember that they took this land from the Indians. And just as much as it's theirs, it's ours too now. We've got to stand up.

The best thing that we can do for Mr. Chaney, for Mickey Schwerner, for Andrew Goodman is stand up and demand our rights. All these people here who are not registered voters should be in line Monday morning from one corner of this county to the next, demanding, don't ask if I can become a registered voter. Demand! Say, "Baby, I'm here!"

Don't just look at me and the people here and go back and say that you've been to a nice service, a lot of people came, there were a lot of hot-blasted newsmen around, anything like that. . . . I'm going to tell you deep down in my heart what I feel right now. If you do go back home and sit down and take it, God damn your souls!

Don't bow down anymore! Hold your heads up!

We want our freedom now! I don't want to have to go to another memorial. I'm tired of funerals, tired of 'em! We've got to stand up.

33

FRED DUTTON

Memorandum to Bill Moyers concerning the Mississippi Delegation Problem

August 10, 1964

Presidential aide Fred Dutton drafted a memo to President Johnson's close adviser Bill Moyers about "the Mississippi delegation problem." In addition to setting out the various arguments for and against the challenge, Dutton framed the memo in terms of Johnson's nomination and election. This approach to the challenge would make compromise, or even negotiations, between the administration and the delegation difficult. President Johnson fancied himself as a strong ally of the civil rights movement, and he had the record to prove it. How do you account for his failure to support the Freedom Democrats against the white supremacist state delegation?

You may be interested in the attached summary of the Mississippi delegation problem. I had the memorandum put together so that we could see all the arguments on one short piece of paper.

SUBJECT: MISSISSIPPI DELEGATION PROBLEM

Arguments That May Be Raised by the Competing Mississippi Delegations

I. By the Freedom Democratic Party

    A. The Mississippi regulars do not meet the criteria set forth in the Call for the 1964 Democratic Convention:

        1. They do not undertake to ensure that voters in Mississippi will have the opportunity to cast their election ballots for

---

Memo with attachment, Fred Dutton to Bill Moyers, August 10, 1964, "Gen PL 1/ST 24 11/22/63–8/21/64," WHCF, box 81, LBJ Library.

the Presidential and Vice Presidential nominees selected by the Democratic National Convention.

2. They are not bona fide Democrats who have the interests, welfare and success of the Democratic Party at heart.

B. The Mississippi regulars have not complied with Mississippi law:

1. They have barred the Freedom Democrats from precinct, county, and state meetings of the regular party.

2. In some parts of the state they have failed to hold statutorily required meetings.

C. The Mississippi regular party is in violation of the Federal Constitution:

1. Negroes are systematically excluded from registering with the party.

D. The Freedom Democratic Party has complied to the extent possible with the Mississippi law.

E. The Freedom Democratic Party meets the criteria set forth in the Call for the 1964 Democratic Convention.

F. The Freedom Democratic Party is open to all Mississippians.

II. By the Mississippi "Regulars"

A. The Freedom Democratic Party is not qualified to represent Mississippi because it has not complied with Mississippi law:

1. It is not a registered party.

2. It is not entitled to use the word "Democratic" in its name.

3. It may not have held conventions in enough counties within the state.

B. The Mississippi regulars have traditionally done their job, and they are not now pledged to vote for someone other than the Presidential and Vice Presidential nominees selected by the Democratic National Convention.

C. The Mississippi regulars represent a majority of the registered Democratic voters in Mississippi.

Pitfalls to Avoid in Determining a Course of Action

1. Weakening our civil rights image.
2. Having delegations walk out. If some do walk out, our decision should try to minimize that number.
3. Inquiring into the legality of other state delegations.
4. Having one of the Mississippi delegations seek a temporary restraining order against the convention while petitioning a court for a hearing on the merits.
5. An extended floor debate which is bound to become bitter and which could only place Governor Sanders and his two Negro delegates in embarrassing positions.
6. Physical violence on the Convention floor.
7. Encouraging massive civil rights demonstrations in Atlantic City and throughout the country.

5

The Atlantic City Challenge

34

LEE WHITE

Memorandum for the President on Dr. King and the Freedom Democratic Party Challenge
August 13, 1964

Dr. Martin Luther King Jr. and several other movement leaders sought to meet with President Lyndon Johnson to talk about the Mississippi Freedom Democratic Party challenge. President Johnson referred them to his adviser, Lee White. In his meeting with White, King linked the MFDP challenge to the civil rights movement as a whole and also to the president's election prospects.

I talked to King at about 6:45 p.m. and told him of my earlier conversation with Rustin. . . .

He said . . . that there were some points which he believed should be made to the President concerning the importance of the Mississippi "Freedom Party" effort to be seated. He described Goldwater's candidacy as a threat to the Nation and recognized that, wittingly or unwittingly, he would attempt to capitalize on the white backlash. He said

Memo, Lee White to the President, "Conversation with Martin Luther King," August 13, 1964, attached to note [from Lee White?], "Deke DeLoach called me," August 19, 1964, "Ex PL 1/ST 24 Seating Mississippi Delegation at the Democratic National Convention," WHCF, box 81, LBJ Library.

that it is becoming increasingly difficult to hold down demonstrations and riots and that unless some sort of satisfactory adjustment of the "Freedom Party" issue is found, he was fearful that the intensity and the number of the demonstrations would be detrimental to the President's November prospects. He also pointed out that he was aware of the political arguments about not alienating southern states, but expressed the hope that some compromise might be developed which would hold down any southern white resentment and still keep the Negro morale from a disastrous decline. He believes that in many states Negro voters may make the difference, and mentioned Georgia and Tennessee specifically. He expressed some concern that Negroes could gain the impression that the outcome of the election really made no difference to them and that they might therefore stay at home.

King said that he felt a moral obligation to bring these points to the attention of the President personally.

35

Johnson Tapes concerning Freedom Summer
1964

U.S. presidents began secretly recording meetings and phone conversations in 1940 and continued this practice until 1978. In these brief excerpts from private conversations, President Johnson's understanding of the politics of civil rights becomes clear. Here he discusses the challenges of dealing with the MFDP. In this document collection, you have the chance to compare the advice given to President Johnson by his confidants on these matters with the actual words he spoke in frank and private conversations. How did the advice the president received differ from his own perspectives? How should historians use the conversation of presidents in conjunction with the memos of their trusted advisers?

Michael R. Beschloss, ed., *Taking Charge: The Johnson White House Tapes, 1963–1964* (New York: Simon and Schuster, 1997), 466, 467, 470–71, 510–11, 514–17, 520–21, 524–27, 534–35.

Thursday, July 23, 1964

JOHN CONNALLY

5:31 P.M.

LBJ: I don't know how anybody can stop what they're doing on the Freedom Party. I think it's very bad and I wish that I could stop it. I tried, but I haven't been able to. . . . It may very well be that Bobby has started it. Last night I couldn't sleep. About two-thirty I waked up. And I tried to figure what I would do if I were a candidate for Vice President . . . and the bossman would say that "I can't take you on account of the South." I think the first thing I'd do is try to make the South of no value either to him or to me. . . . I believe that's what is happening. . . . Joe Rauh and Martin Luther King and folks that normally run with that crowd are leading 'em. Humphrey is trying his best to put an end to it, but he hasn't had much luck with 'em. . . .

LBJ: I just shudder to think what would happen if Goldwater won it. He's a man that's had two nervous breakdowns. He's not a stable fellow at all. . . .

CONNALLY: [laughs]

LBJ: I don't really know how to handle it all. That's the honest truth.

CONNALLY: Oh yes, you do.

LBJ: No, I don't. . . . If I win, I lose. Because I want the South for me. . . . And if I can't offer the ticket the South, I haven't got really anything to offer them. I don't have any standing in Chicago . . . Iowa, Los Angeles, New York City. . . . Now my judgment is we're gonna lose every Southern state, including Kentucky and Oklahoma and Missouri. . . . I just don't think they can take this nigra stuff. . . .

CONNALLY: Yeah, I think they will. . . .

LBJ: I don't know. . . . If this . . . fight against the South gets up, I'm gonna wind up without anything but the South. And the South ain't gonna be for me. But *they're* not gonna be for me on grounds that I'm a Southerner. Because I have no real rapport or anything in common with those folks. The only thing is I got possession of the office at the moment. . . .

Sunday, August 9, 1964

WALTER REUTHER

8:50 A.M.

LBJ: If you and Hubert Humphrey have got any leadership, you'd get Joe Rauh off that damn television. The only thing that can really screw us good is to seat that group of challengers from Mississippi. . . . He said he's going to take it to the convention floor. Now there's not a damn vote that we get by seating these folks. What we want to do is elect some Congressmen to keep 'em from repealing this act. And who's seated at this convention don't amount to a damn. Only reason I would let Mississippi come in is because I don't want to run off fourteen border states, like Oklahoma and like Kentucky. . . . Incidentally this Governor has done everything I've asked him to do in Mississippi. We've broken that case. I talk to him two or three times a week. Now he's not for Johnson. But I can't say that he hasn't listened to us and he hasn't cooperated.

REUTHER: Exactly. . . . We'll lose Mississippi, but the impact on the other Southern states—

LBJ: That's all I'm worried about. . . . I've got to carry Georgia. . . . I've got to carry Texas. . . . We don't want to cut off our nose to spite our face. If they give us four years, I'll guarantee the Freedom delegation somebody representing views like that will be seated four years from now. But we can't do it all before breakfast. . . .

Friday, August 14, 1964

HUBERT HUMPHREY

11:05 A.M.

HUMPHREY: I've been just working the devil out of that Joe. . . . And I understood that . . . Joe had quite a talk . . . on the basis of seating both of these delegations.

LBJ: You can't do that at all. There's no compromise. You can seat one or the other. You can't seat both of them because if you do, then the other one walks out. There's just no justification for messing with the Freedom Party at all in Mississippi. . . . Your labor union people . . . are upset. Think that nigra's going to get his job.

HUMPHREY: Yeah.

LBJ: . . . They think a nigra's going to move next door to them. . . . And our organizations are tired and worn out and lazy and looking after themselves. They just think they've got labor and nigras and that's all there is to it. We're not appealing to the fresh people. So this is an extremely dangerous election. Now the thing that makes it more dangerous than anything else is—I am telling you, if I know anything I know this—if we mess with the group of Negroes that were elected to nothing, that met in a hotel room . . . and throw out the Governor and elected officials of the state—if we mess with them, we will lose fifteen states without even campaigning. . . .

LBJ: We've got to do something that will convince the CORE crowd and Martin Luther King and Joe Rauh that if they want to help Goldwater, okay, they can go this way. . . . They'll have a roll call. The Northern states will probably prevail. New York and Pennsylvania and California and Ohio and Michigan cannot afford to have it said that they are for the Governor of Mississippi . . . against the Negroes in their own town, where they've got 20 percent Negroes.

HUMPHREY: That's right.

LBJ: . . . So we throw them out. And when we do, we write a blank check to him for fifteen states. . . .

HUMPHREY: I don't have as much control or influence with these people as I would like. . . . I have been in touch with Farmer. I haven't been in touch lately with King.

LBJ: King has gone to Europe today. His man Rustin is calling. They are demanding that this be made the big fish. . . .

LBJ: Try to see if the Negroes don't realize that they've got the President, they'll have the Vice President, they've got the law, they'll have the government for four years. . . . Why in the living hell do they want to hand—*shovel*—Goldwater fifteen states? . . .

HUMPHREY: . . . We're just not dealing with . . . emotionally stable people on this, Mr. President.

Friday, August 21, 1964

WALTER JENKINS

8:30 P.M.

LBJ: I think you ought to call Humphrey . . . and say, "You better get Reuther and you better get Rauh and quit causing these goddamn troubles, Hubert, because this is going to make a bad convention if you don't tell them to quit doing stuff like this. Now if you haven't got any influence with any of this ADA crowd, tell us who has."

Monday, August 24, 1964

RICHARD RUSSELL

11:10 A.M.

RUSSELL: I heard King addressing that crowd down there on the Boardwalk. . . . I heard him on my car radio coming down here, and he was just openly threatening. I don't see how you can possibly do business with a man—black, white, green, or yellow—that just comes out and intimidates. Says, "Don't do this, we are going to take it out of your hide." He said on the radio, "They say we niggers haven't got anywhere else to go. We'll show them we *have* got somewhere else to go."

LBJ: Yes, he's been saying that in private. . . . The question is what you do when they are getting ready to take charge of the convention. . . .

RUSSELL: You don't do a thing but say you're sorry, you think they are ill-advised. . . . Undoubtedly there may have been irregularities in selecting the white delegation, but . . . this Freedom delegation . . . didn't have . . . conventions but in about eighteen or twenty counties. . . . I don't see how the hell they claim they represent the state. . . . It ain't going to hurt you any in the country to get run over. It would hurt your pride like hell, I know, but it isn't going to hurt you politically.

LBJ: I would think that they'd say that hell, the Negroes have got more power in the Democratic party than the President has, and the damned nigras are taking it over—and to hell with the Democratic party.

RUSSELL: It would increase the backlash a little bit. No question about that—whatever the backlash is. But this is August. It's over two months before the election. . . .

LBJ: I don't think there's any question but what Martin Luther King and that group wants me to be in a position of giving them an excuse to say that I have turned on the Negro.

RUSSELL: I don't believe they can sell that to the *Negro* even.

WALTER JENKINS

Approximately 4:30 P.M.

JENKINS: [Hubert Humphrey] said, "I'm a hell of a salesman. I walked into the lion's den. . . . I argued fervently. I used all the heartstrings that I had and I made no headway. . . . I think we can forget now any possibility of them not trying for a floor fight unless they have some votes." He said he asked some of the people there the result of giving them two votes. . . . Texas, Georgia, Florida, North Carolina would stay. Arkansas, Louisiana doubtful. . . . He says he's racked his brain for anything further to do. He's not making a suggestion that you get into it. But he says this fellow [Aaron] Henry is quite intelligent—he's more reasonable than some. . . .

LBJ: [upset] I don't want to see 'em at all. . . . If they're interested in the slightest in what concerns me, it is to go on and take the compromise that Rauh proposed. That's what they ought to do. . . . If they want Goldwater, they can have Goldwater.

WALTER REUTHER

8:25 P.M.

LBJ: [Clark Clifford] and Abe [Fortas] are . . . just distressed beyond words.

REUTHER: I am too. I'm going to get in there and see if I can't help get ahold of this damned thing.

LBJ: I think the Negroes are going back to the Reconstruction period. Going right where they were then. They set themselves back a hundred years.

REUTHER: They're completely irrational. They don't know the victory they got is the proposition that next time no one can discriminate against Negroes. . . .

LBJ: And then I'm just trying to get a Vice President for 'em. And I want to try to get him accepted by the country. . . . I don't know why they don't let us do it. . . . Hell, the Northerners are more upset about this. They call me and wire me, Walter . . . that the Negroes have taken over the country. They're running the White House. They're running the Democratic party. And it's not Mississippi and Alabama. . . . You're catching your hell from Michigan, Ohio, Philadelphia, and New York! . . . They're before that television. They don't understand that nearly every white man in this country would be frightened if he thought the Negroes were gonna take him over. . . . But they're on the television showing it. We can't ever buy spots that will equal this. We've got five million dollars budgeted, but we can't undo what they've done in the last two days—unless you do it tomorrow.

Tuesday, August 25, 1964

HUBERT HUMPHREY AND WALTER REUTHER

2:31 P.M.

REUTHER: Hubert and I have got a meeting set up at three-thirty with Dr. King and this fellow [Aaron] Henry and I think we can . . . get this . . . fight off the television cameras. . . . We can all leave here together united and go back and do the hard work of winning this election behind your leadership.

HUMPHREY: Mr. President . . . we're not going to meet with Dr. Luther King or anybody else to negotiate. . . . We've taken a position now. . . . We know it's right.

LBJ: Did you talk to any of their people about this?

REUTHER: Yes, we have had some informal talks. . . . But I am confident that we can reduce the opposition to this to a microscopic faction so that they'll be completely unimportant. . . .

LBJ: [immensely relieved] I think it's a good solution. . . . Our party's always been a group that you can come to with any bellyache and injustice, whether it was a pecan-shelling plant that paid four cents an hour or sweatshop wages or usurious interest rates or discrimination to vote or Ku Klux Klan whipping somebody. . . . That's what the Democratic party's for. That's why it was born. And that's why it survives. . . . Long as the poor and the downtrodden and the bended know that they can come to us and be heard. And that's what we're doing. We're hearing 'em. . . . We passed a law back there in '57 and said it was the first time in eighty-five years that everyone was going to have a chance to vote. . . . And we're going to say it again in the convention in '64. . . . Get ahold of these people and say to 'em, "For God's sakes, we've tasted from the cup of injustice ourselves. . . . You're going to have a President and . . . a Vice President . . . that you trust. You're going to have Congress. . . . Let's all get out there in the precincts . . . we'll start out next January and do enough about . . . economic and social and other interests that we can go in there and send a fellow like Humphrey down to make a speech now and then and cry with 'em a little."

36

FANNIE LOU HAMER

Remarks before the Credentials Committee
August 22, 1964

*In less than ten minutes, Fannie Lou Hamer described the living condi-
tions of black people in Mississippi and the challenges they faced as they
attempted to participate in the political system. The strength of the MFDP
convention challenge was the power of local people to give voice to their
experiences. What kinds of reprisals did Mrs. Hamer face for trying to
register to vote? Why was her testimony so powerful in making the claim
for seating the Freedom Democrats?*

CHAIRMAN LAWRENCE: In other words, we are here for the purpose of this
Convention, and for the purpose of the election of delegates and the
seating of delegates, and the future conduct of the Party in the state. I
think we can save a lot of time if we didn't have repetitious testimony
on the same subject.

MR. RAUH: If Your Honor please—

CHAIRMAN LAWRENCE: How many minutes have you got?

MR. LEVENTHAL: I have given him 17 minutes.

MR. RAUH: If Your Honor please, I must respectfully disagree. It is the
very terror that these people are living through that is the reason that
Negroes aren't voting. They are kept out of the Democratic Party by
the terror of the regular party and what I want the Credentials Committee to hear is the terror which the regular party uses on the people
of Mississippi which is what Reverend King was explaining, which is
what Aaron Henry was explaining and which is what the next witness
will explain, Mrs. Fannie Lou Hamer.

William Heath Papers, box 6, folder 24.

Remarks of Mrs. Fannie Lou Hamer

MRS. HAMER: Mr. Chairman, and the Credentials Committee, my name is Mrs. Fannie Lou Hamer, and I live at 626 East Lafayette Street, Ruleville, Mississippi, Sunflower County, the home of Senator James O. Eastland, and Senator Stennis.

It was the 31st of August in 1962 that 18 of us traveled 26 miles to the county courthouse in Indianola to try to register to try to become first-class citizens.

We was met in Indianola by Mississippi men, Highway Patrolmen, and they only allowed two of us in to take the literacy test at the time. After we had taken this test and started back to Ruleville, we was held up by the City Police and the State Highway Patrolmen and carried back to Indianola where the bus driver was charged that day with driving a bus the wrong color.

After we paid the fine among us, we continued on to Ruleville, and Reverend Jeff Sunny carried me four miles in the rural area where I had worked as a timekeeper and sharecropper for 18 years. I was met there by my children, who told me the plantation owner was angry because I had gone down to try to register.

After they told me, my husband came, and said the plantation owner was raising cain because I had tried to register, and before he quit talking the plantation owner came, and said, "Fanny Lou, do you know—did Pap tell you what I said?"

And I said, "Yes, sir."

"I mean that," he said. "If you don't go down and withdraw your registration, you will have to leave," said, "Then if you go down and withdraw," he said, "You will—you might have to go because we are not ready for that in Mississippi."

And I addressed him and told him and said "I didn't try to register for you. I tried to register for myself."

I had to leave that same night.

On the 10th of September, 1962, 16 bullets was fired into the home of Mr. and Mrs. Robert Tucker for me. That same night two girls were shot in Ruleville, Mississippi. Also Mr. Joe McDonald's house was shot in.

And in June, the 9th, 1963, I had attended a voter registration workshop, was returning back to Mississippi. Ten of us was traveling by the Continental Trailway bus. When we got to Winona, Mississippi, which is Montgomery County, four of the people got off to use the washroom, and two of the people—to use the restaurant—two of the people wanted to use the washroom.

The four people that had gone in to use the restaurant was ordered out. During this time I was on the bus. But when I looked through the window and saw they had rushed out I got off of the bus to see what had happened, and one of the ladies said, "It was a State Highway Patrolman and a Chief of Police ordered us out."

I got back on the bus and one of the persons [who] had used the washroom got back on the bus, too.

As soon as I was seated on the bus, I saw when they began to get the four people in a highway patrolman's car. I stepped off of the bus to see what was happening and somebody screamed from the car that the four workers was in and said, "Get that one there," and when I went to get in the car, when the man told me I was under arrest, he kicked me.

I was carried to the county jail, and put in the booking room. They left some of the people in the booking room and began to place us in cells. I was placed in a cell with a young woman called Miss Euvester Simpson. After I was placed in the cell I began to hear sounds of licks and screams. I could hear the sounds of licks and horrible screams, and I could hear somebody say, "Can you say, yes, sir, nigger? Can you say yes, sir?"

And they would say other horrible names.

She would say, "Yes, I can say yes, sir."

"So, say it."

She says, "I don't know you well enough."

They beat her, I don't know how long, and after a while she began to pray, and asked God to have mercy on those people.

And it wasn't too long before three white men came to my cell. One of these men was a State Highway Patrolman and he asked me where I was from, and I told him Ruleville, he said, "We are going to check this."

And they left my cell and it wasn't too long before they came back. He said, "You are from Ruleville all right," and he used a curse word, and he said, "We are going to make you wish you was dead."

I was carried out of that cell into another cell where they had two Negro prisoners. The State Highway Patrolman ordered the first Negro to take the blackjack.

The first Negro prisoner ordered me, by orders from the State Highway Patrolman for me, to lay down on a bunk bed on my face, and I laid on my face.

The first Negro began to beat, and I was beat by the first Negro until he was exhausted, and I was holding my hands behind me at that time on my left side because I suffered from polio when I was six years old.

After the first Negro had beat until he was exhausted the State Highway Patrolman ordered the second Negro to take the blackjack.

The second Negro began to beat and I began to work my feet, and the State Highway Patrolman ordered the first Negro who had beat to set on my feet to keep me from working my feet. I began to scream and one white man got up and began to beat me in my head and tell me to hush.

One white man—my dress had worked up high—he walked over and pulled my dress—I pulled my dress down and he pulled my dress back up.

I was in jail when Medgar Evers was murdered.

All of this is on account we want to register, to become first-class citizens, and if the Freedom Democratic Party is not seated now, I question America, is this America, the land of the free and the home of the brave where we have to sleep with our telephones off of the hooks because our lives be threatened daily because we want to live as decent human beings, in America?

Thank you.

(Applause)

37

JOE RAUH

Letter to Leslie McLemore

June 15, 1965

In 1965, as a new graduate student studying political science at Atlanta University, Leslie Burl McLemore, a former SNCC field secretary, a founder of the Mississippi Freedom Democratic Party, and a delegate to the Democratic National Convention, wrote to Joseph Rauh to solicit his opinion on the compromise offered by the Democratic Party at the Atlantic City convention. Rauh was lead counsel for the United Automobile

Joseph L. Rauh Papers, Manuscript Division, Library of Congress, Washington, D.C., container 86. Hereafter cited, Joseph L. Rauh Papers.

Workers, a prominent Democratic Party activist, and a strong supporter of the civil rights movement. He was hired by the MFDP to serve as their chief counsel. The Atlantic City convention was not his first experience at the highest levels of political decision making: He was also a close confidant of President Johnson and Senator Hubert Humphrey. In his response to McLemore, Rauh remembers the Atlantic City challenge as an unqualified success and notes in particular that the actions of the MFDP helped lay the foundation for the successful passage of the 1965 Voting Rights Act. How did Rauh's experience as a labor leader and political operative influence his understanding of the challenge and also, possibly, his conduct?

This is in reply to your letter of June 9 asking my opinion on the MFDP's stand at Atlantic City last summer. I am happy to respond.

I believe the MFDP scored a great success at Atlantic City—a success far beyond anything that could reasonably have been anticipated a month or two earlier. There were many facets of this success. The MFDP struggle at Atlantic City aroused the nation to an understanding of the disgraceful political situation in Mississippi and to a considerable degree laid the basis for the present highly significant Voting Rights Act of 1965. The MFDP drove the "regular" Mississippi delegation from the Convention. The MFDP was formally (albeit partially) recognized by the Convention through the offer of seats to Aaron Henry and Ed King. Finally, and probably most importantly, the MFDP struggle changed the rules of the Democratic Convention so that never again will a group of delegates discriminatingly chosen be seated in a Democratic Convention.

This monumental achievement resulted from many factors. One was the magnificent presentations of Aaron Henry, Ed King and Mrs. Hamer at the hearing before the Credentials Committee. Another was the work of the MFDP staff. A third was the unity of the civil rights movement evidenced by the testimony before the Credentials Committee of Roy Wilkins, Martin Luther King, Jim Farmer, and Jay Moore and their help in rounding up delegate support. Other factors may have been involved, too.

I have never felt overly critical of the failure of the MFDP to accept the tremendous success which I think they won. I did, of course, favor accepting the proposal of the Convention (although I signed a statement that the MFDP was "entitled" to more), but I could understand why it was hard for MFDP to accept any compromise, even a favorable one. In fighting for the MFDP at the Convention, I had to make tough demands and optimistic statements. As in a labor union collective bargaining situation, one has to ask for far more than one could possibly expect to get. The difficulty in doing this is that you steam up your troops so that it is hard for them to take less than what is demanded. Yet, if you don't steam up your forces, you can't get anything at all. I believe this dilemma was at the root of the problem at Atlantic City.

My criticism of the MFDP at Atlantic City lies in their failure to hold a rational discussion of the compromise the afternoon it was adopted by the Credentials Committee. Having wrung significant concessions from the Convention with the support of civil rights leaders like those named and Rustin, and others, these leaders were certainly entitled to participate in the decision on what to do with those concessions. Worse yet was the use by the MFDP people and especially the staff of words like "sell-out," "double-dealing," et cetera—words that are still being used. There was no sell-out or double-dealing; a very high degree of integrity was shown at Atlantic City by people in very difficult roles. And the highest award for integrity to my mind goes to Vice President Humphrey. Many times at Atlantic City I heard that I was destroying Humphrey's chance to be Vice President by my fight for the MFDP. Yet, despite our 17 years of close political association, Humphrey never once asked me for a single concession to help him win the high post he now holds.

I look back on Atlantic City as a great experience. If I have any sorrow about an affair, it is the bitterness that Bob Moses and others showed there and since. But this too, I believe, time will dull.

I remember the August day in Jackson when you were elected Vice Chairman of the MFDP. Congratulations again and with all good wishes.

Sincerely Yours,
Joseph L. Rauh, Jr.

38

AARON E. HENRY

Position Paper on the Rejection of the Compromise
August 29, 1964

Aaron E. Henry was the state president of the NAACP and chairman of the Council of Federated Organizations. He also served as the head of the MFDP delegation to the Democratic National Convention in Atlantic City. In this document, Henry explains why the MFDP delegates rejected the compromise offered by the national leadership of the Democratic Party. Henry's support for the compromise, and his reassurance that the Freedom Democrats would speak for and support the Johnson-Humphrey ticket, put him at odds with more militant members of the COFO coalition. As you think about the documents on the MFDP, consider carefully how ideals and morality shaped political decision making at Atlantic City.

The participation of the MFDP, just concluded in Atlantic City, focused the attention of the World on the problems of the Negro People in Mississippi. This participation rejected the issue of White America telling Negroes who their leaders will be, and this participation also rejected the idea of tokenism that White America is using all over the Country to silence the Negro demands for freedom. Of the one-thousand and sixty-seven messages, letters, telegrams, etc., 1,011 of these support the MFDP in rejecting the Compromise worked out by the National leadership of the National Democratic Party while 56 thought the Miss. Freedom Democratic Party should have accepted the compromise. This Compromise would have given Aaron E. Henry, Chairman of the Delegation, and Rev. Edwin King, National Committeeman, delegate status, but would deny delegate status to all the other delegates of the MFDP. The MFDP had no choice in selecting to whom the two votes would go. This was decided *for us.*

We went to this Convention armed with the greatest might one could have on his side—the might of truth! We presented the truth and came within one vote in the Credentials Committee of winning all we went

Joseph L. Rauh Papers, container 86, file 2.

to Atlantic City for, and that was to be seated as the Democratic representatives from the State of Mississippi. It took the personal hand of President Lyndon Johnson to keep this vote from our grasp. It was not that the President was against us, however; he took the position that he would lose the states of Texas, Arkansas, Tennessee, and Georgia, in addition to Mississippi and Alabama, if the Convention voted to seat us, we of the Mississippi Freedom Democratic Party. Thus the issue within the Administration was purely political. Our victory on moral and legal grounds was overwhelming.

We have established a liaison between the National Democratic Party and the MFDP which we feel will aid us in correcting the many evils that beset Negro and White Americans who want to be free. Many of our delegates will be accepting speaking engagements all over America, speaking in behalf of President Johnson and Senator Hubert Humphrey for President and Vice-President.

We shall begin immediately to secure the necessary signatures to guarantee the names of the Presidential Electors for Lyndon Johnson and Hubert Humphrey on the ballot for the state of Mississippi. We have instructed our legal Counsel, Attorney Joe Rauh, to proceed immediately to file proceedings quashing the injunction that has been leveled against the MFDP, so that we will have no harassment as we go about our task of helping elect Lyndon Johnson and Hubert Humphrey to the Office of President and Vice-President of the U.S.

We express our appreciation to all of our friends in this fight. Our special appreciation goes to Attorney Joe Rauh, Congresswoman Edith Green of Oregon, Senator Wayne Morris of Oregon, Congressman Phillip Burton of California and the seventeen members of the Credentials Committee who supported our position even when President Johnson said no.

[To] Senator Hubert Humphrey and Mr. Walter Reuther who tried to get the Miss. Freedom delegation to accept the Credentials Committee's report (the compromise?) that seated the all white, racist, disloyal delegation from the state of Miss. and refused to seat us, a delegation pledged to support the Democratic Party ticket with all we have, we say, we are truly sorry that you could not come up with a proposition that our delegation [could] in good conscience accept. We admit to not being politically oriented. Our orientation is based on morality and rightness. This is the only way we know how to fight, and we pray for the day when politics will embrace without reservation, these two factors, so that *we will not only walk in the same direction, but we will walk that way together.*

Our delegates will be happy to speak all over America for the National Democratic Party in our effort and promise, regardless of the outcome of our fight in Atlantic City, that we would come home and work for the election of the National Democratic Ticket. We ask now for your assistance in relieving local harassment by local white Officials so that this can be done.

In the meantime let us work together from now until 1968 to make sure that by then the National Democratic Party will have purged itself of all evils pertaining to race, religion or national origin of Americans who are seeking the opportunity to participate in the National Democratic Party.

A special commendation to all of the friends and Organizations that supported us including NAACP, CORE, SNCC, SCLC, and the National Council of Churches. Without your support we could not have fought the good fight.

39

COUNCIL OF FEDERATED ORGANIZATIONS

To All Friends of the MFDP

1964

This memorandum outlines the Mississippi movement's plans for the future. Although Mississippi's "closed society" was cracking open, much work remained to be done. The goal of voting rights had not been secured, the impact of the Civil Rights Act of 1964 was not yet fully implemented, and the problems of poverty and inequality persisted. How would you describe the tone of this memo? Why did the leaders of the MFDP believe it was necessary to explain their rejection of the compromise to their friends?

We are enclosing a report explaining the role of the MFDP at the Convention in Atlantic City and the plans of the MFDP for the future. We hope that this report will help you understand more fully the position and focus of the MFDP.

CORE Papers, reel 45, frame 295.

As the Convention made clear, there are many things that you in the North can do to help the MFDP. There is the obvious and omnipresent need for money and supplies.

In the next few weeks we will be running 5 campaigns for Senate and the House of Representatives. And poverty in Mississippi means not only that people are poor, but that they have no money with which to help themselves. We must have material support from outside the state if we are to keep pace with the growing strength of organization among the people themselves.

We also need political support. Because we had that support, we made the Democratic National Convention stand still for four days, and received the coverage in press and television we so vitally needed. But we lost the battle at the Convention.

Now we are working to challenge the Mississippi representatives to Senate and the Congress. If we are to win this battle against the Regular Democratic Party of Mississippi, we must have pressure from you on the President and on the representatives of the National Democratic Party in your state.

But it is most important to remember that the members of the MFDP are Mississippi Negroes first and foremost, and it is this condition that shapes their lives. Unless the state itself changes, their lives cannot improve—and the state will not change without pressure from the rest of the country.

You must help by making sure the people of the MFDP are not forgotten, by insisting that the story of Mississippi continue to be told, and by calling for the kind of Federal presence that will bring Freedom to those people's lives.

A Chronology of Events Related to Freedom Summer (1944–1965)

1944   The Supreme Court outlaws the white primary (*Smith v. Allwright*).

1951   The Regional Council of Negro Leadership is founded in Mound Bayou, Mississippi.

1954   *May*   The Supreme Court declares separate educational facilities unconstitutional (*Brown v. Board of Education*).

Medgar Evers becomes the first NAACP field secretary for Mississippi.

The white Citizens' Council is formed in Indianola, Mississippi.

1955   *August*   Fourteen-year-old Emmett Till murdered by two white men.

Rev. George Lee and Lamar Smith are killed because of their voter registration work.

1960   Sit-ins begin in Greensboro, North Carolina.

1961   The Congress of Racial Equality (CORE) initiates freedom rides.

Clarie Collins Harvey forms Womanpower Unlimited in Jackson, Mississippi.

The Student Nonviolent Coordinating Committee (SNCC) launches a voter registration project in McComb, Mississippi.

1962   *February*   The Council of Federated Organizations (COFO) is founded by major civil rights organizations operating in Mississippi.

SNCC begins a voter registration project in the Mississippi Delta.

August   Fannie Lou Hamer is evicted from the W. D. Marlow plantation.

October   After a protracted legal battle and rioting by white supremacists, James Meredith becomes the first black student to register for classes at the University of Mississippi.

1963 *June*   Medgar Evers is gunned down in his carport by a member of the Citizens' Council.

Fall   Freedom vote held.

Winter   Members of COFO debate whether to invite whites to work in Mississippi.

1964 *June*   Orientation sessions are held for Freedom Summer volunteers in Oxford, Ohio.

Three civil rights workers are murdered in Neshoba County.

Freedom Summer begins.

July 2   President Lyndon Johnson signs the Civil Rights Act.

August 4   The bodies of the three murdered civil rights workers are discovered in an earthen dam.

August 6   The Mississippi Freedom Democratic Party holds its state convention in Jackson.

August 22   The Democratic National Convention begins in Atlantic City, New Jersey.

August 25   Freedom Democrats reject the two-seat compromise at the national convention.

1965 *January*   Freedom Democrats challenge the legitimacy of the all-white Mississippi congressional delegation.

August   President Johnson signs the Voting Rights Act.

Questions for Consideration

1. Stokely Carmichael (Kwame Ture) argued that the Mississippi summer project was a turning point for an entire generation of activists. What evidence can you find in the introduction and the documents to support his assessment?

2. What was the impact of the *Brown v. Board of Education* decision on Mississippi whites and blacks?

3. How did the presence of Bob Moses affect the planning and execution of the summer project?

4. Why were organizations such as the NAACP, SCLC, SNCC, and CORE able to cooperate with one another in Mississippi in the early 1960s?

5. How does a focus on local people and local movements help us understand the scope and significance of Freedom Summer?

6. What do the documents reveal about the role of the federal government in the Mississippi movement? Why might the federal government have played the role it did?

7. What do the documents reveal about how Mississippi whites responded to the announcement and implementation of Freedom Summer? Why might Mississippi whites have responded as they did?

8. In the debates within COFO, who supported the summer project? Why? Who opposed the project? Why? Why did COFO decide to move forward with the project?

9. How did COFO prepare for Freedom Summer? What does this reveal about the summer project? What does it reveal about the civil rights movement? Based on Documents 10 to 15, what can you learn about Freedom Summer by the way COFO prepared for it?

10. What do the documents reveal about the challenges and opportunities associated with the decision to bring hundreds of northern white volunteers into a southern black-led movement?

11. Why did the planners of Freedom Summer decide to operate freedom schools? Why did they decide to launch a voter registration campaign? How were freedom schools related to the voter registration campaign?

12. What do the introduction and the documents reveal about the ultimate purpose of the freedom schools?

13. What did the freedom schools accomplish?

14. What do the introduction and the documents reveal about the recruitment and orientation of summer volunteers?

15. How did the murders of James Chaney, Andrew Goodman, and Michael Schwerner affect the Freedom Summer volunteers? How did the murders affect black Mississippians? How did the murders affect U.S. politics?

16. Identify the different kinds of volunteers. What characteristics did the organizers look for in the volunteers? What does this exercise suggest about COFO and the summer project?

17. The Mississippi Freedom Democratic Party is often understood as a parallel institution. What is a parallel institution? Why did civil rights activists find parallel institutions useful and attractive in their efforts to challenge segregation?

18. What was the compromise offered to the Mississippi Freedom Democratic Party, why was it rejected, and how did it impact the struggle for a voting rights law?

19. What did the Mississippi Freedom Democratic Party accomplish? Which of its goals did it achieve? Which of its goals did it fail to achieve? Why didn't it achieve all of its goals?

Selected Bibliography

Belfrage, Sally. *Freedom Summer.* New York: Viking, 1965.

Blackwell, Unita, with Joanne Prichard Morris. *Barefootin': Life Lessons from the Road to Freedom.* New York: Crown Press, 2006.

Bolton, Charles C. *The Hardest Deal of All: The Battle over School Integration in Mississippi.* Jackson: University Press of Mississippi, 2005.

Cagin, Seth, and Philip Dray. *We Are Not Afraid: The Story of Goodman, Schwerner, and Chaney and the Civil Rights Campaign for Mississippi.* New York: Nation Books, 2006.

Cobb, Charles E., Jr. *This Nonviolent Stuff'll Get You Killed: How Guns Made the Civil Rights Movement Possible.* New York: Basic Books, 2014.

Cobb, James C. *The Most Southern Place on Earth: The Mississippi Delta and the Roots of Southern Identity.* New York: Oxford University Press, 1992.

Crespino, Joseph. *In Search of Another Country: Mississippi and the Conservative Counterrevolution.* Princeton, N.J.: Princeton University Press, 2007.

Crosby, Emilye. *A Little Taste of Freedom: The Black Freedom Struggle in Claiborne County, Mississippi.* Chapel Hill: University of North Carolina Press, 2005.

Curry, Constance. *Silver Rights.* Chapel Hill: Algonquin Press, 1995.

Danielson, Chris. *After Freedom Summer: How Race Realigned Mississippi Politics, 1965–1986.* Gainesville: University Press of Florida, 2011.

Dittmer, John. *The Good Doctors: The Medical Committee for Human Rights and the Struggle for Social Justice in Health Care.* New York: Bloomsbury Press, 2009.

———. *Local People: The Struggle for Civil Rights in Mississippi.* Urbana: University of Illinois Press, 1994.

Eagles, Charles. *The Price of Defiance: James Meredith and the Integration of Ole Miss.* Chapel Hill: University of North Carolina Press, 2009.

Erenrich, Susie, ed. *Freedom Is a Constant Struggle: An Anthology of the Mississippi Civil Rights Movement.* Washington, D.C.: Cultural Center for Social Change, 1999.

Evers, Mrs. Medgar, with William Peters. *For Us, the Living.* Garden City, N.Y.: Doubleday, 1967.

Evers-Williams, Myrlie, and Manning Marable. *The Autobiography of Medgar Evers: A Hero's Life and Legacy Revealed through His Writings, Letters, and Speeches.* New York: Basic Books, 2005.

Hamlin, Francoise N. *Crossroads at Clarksdale: The Black Freedom Struggle in the Mississippi Delta after World War II.* Chapel Hill: University of North Carolina Press, 2012.

Henry, Aaron, with Constance Curry. *Aaron Henry: The Fire Ever Burning.* Jackson: University Press of Mississippi, 2000.

Herron, Matt. *Mississippi Eyes: The Story and Photography of the Southern Documentary Project.* Jackson: University Press of Mississippi, 2014.

Horn, Teena F., Alan Huffman, and John Griffin Jones, eds. *Lines Were Drawn: Remembering Court-Ordered Integration at a Mississippi High School.* Jackson: University Press of Mississippi, 2016.

Hudson, Winson, with Constance Curry. *Mississippi Harmony: Memoirs of a Freedom Fighter.* Jackson: University Press of Mississippi, 2004.

Katagiri, Yasuhiro. *The Mississippi State Sovereignty Commission: Civil Rights and States' Rights.* Jackson: University Press of Mississippi, 2001.

King, Ed, and Trent Watts. *Ed King's Mississippi: Behind the Scenes of Freedom Summer.* Jackson: University Press of Mississippi, 2014.

Lee, Chana Kai. *For Freedom's Sake: The Life of Fannie Lou Hamer.* Urbana: University of Illinois Press, 1999.

Mars, Florence. *Witness in Philadelphia.* Baton Rouge: Louisiana State University Press, 1977.

Marsh, Charles. *God's Long Summer: Stories of Faith and Civil Rights.* Princeton, N.J.: Princeton University Press, 1997.

Martinez, Elizabeth, ed. *Letters from Mississippi.* Brookline, Mass.: Zephyr Press edition, 2007.

McAdam, Doug. *Freedom Summer.* New York: Oxford University Press, 1988.

McMillen, Neil R. *The Citizens' Council: Organized Resistance to the Second Reconstruction, 1954–1964.* Urbana: University of Illinois Press, 1971.

———. *Dark Journey: Black Mississippians in the Age of Jim Crow.* Urbana: University of Illinois Press, 1989.

Mills, Kay. *This Little Light of Mine: The Life of Fannie Lou Hamer.* New York: Penguin Press, 1993.

Moody, Anne. *Coming of Age in Mississippi.* New York: Bantam Dell, 1968.

Morris, Tiyi. *Womanpower Unlimited and the Black Freedom Struggle in Mississippi.* Athens: University of Georgia Press, 2015.

Morrison, Minion K. C. *Aaron Henry.* Little Rock: University of Arkansas Press, 2015.

———. *Black Political Mobilization, Leadership, and Power.* Albany: State University of New York Press, 1987.

Moses, Robert P., and Charles E. Cobb Jr. *Radical Equations: Math Literacy and Civil Rights.* Boston: Beacon Press, 2001.

Moye, Todd. *Let the People Decide: Black Freedom and White Resistance Movements in Sunflower County, Mississippi, 1945–1986.* Chapel Hill: University of North Carolina Press, 2004.

O'Brien, M. J. *We Shall Not Be Moved: The Jackson Woolworth's Sit-In and the Movement It Inspired.* Jackson: University Press of Mississippi, 2013.

Parker, Frank. *Black Votes Count: Political Empowerment in Mississippi after 1965.* Chapel Hill: University of North Carolina Press, 1990.

Payne, Charles M. *I've Got the Light of Freedom: The Organizing Tradition and the Mississippi Freedom Struggle.* Berkeley: University of California Press, 1995.

Randall, Herbert, and Bobs M. Tusa. *The Faces of Freedom Summer.* Tuscaloosa: University of Alabama Press, 2001.

Rothschild, Mary Aikin. *A Case of Black and White: Northern Volunteers and the Southern Freedom Summers, 1964–1965.* Westport, Conn.: Greenwood Press, 1982.

Salter, John. *Jackson, Mississippi: An American Chronicle of Struggle and Schism.* Lincoln: University of Nebraska Press, 2011.

Silver, James. *Mississippi: The Closed Society.* Jackson: University Press of Mississippi edition, 2012.

Sojourner, Sue, with Cheryl Reitan. *Thunder of Freedom: Black Leadership and the Transformation of 1960s Mississippi.* Lexington: University Press of Kentucky, 2010.

Sugarman, Tracy. *A Stranger at the Gates: A Summer in Mississippi.* New York: Hill and Wang, 1966.

Todd, Lisa Anderson. *For a Voice and the Vote: My Journey with the Mississippi Freedom Democratic Party.* Lexington: University Press of Kentucky, 2014.

Umoja, Akinyele Omowale. *We Will Shoot Back: Armed Resistance in the Mississippi Freedom Movement.* New York: New York University Press, 2013.

Visser-Maesson, Laura. *Robert Parris Moses: A Life in Civil Rights and Leadership at the Roots.* Chapel Hill: University of North Carolina Press, 2016.

Ward, Jason. *Hanging Bridge: Racial Violence and America's Civil Rights Century.* New York: Oxford University Press, 2016.

Ward, Tom. *Out in the Rural: A Mississippi Health Center and Its War on Poverty.* New York: Oxford University Press, 2016.

Watkins, Hollis, with C. Leigh McInnis. *Brother Hollis: The Sankofa of a Movement Man.* Clinton, Miss.: Sankofa Southern Publishing, 2016.

Watson, Bruce. *Freedom Summer.* New York: Penguin Books, 2010.

Williams, Michael Vinson. *Medgar Evers: Mississippi Martyr.* Fayetteville: University of Arkansas Press, 2011.

Woodruff, Nan E. *American Congo: The African American Freedom Struggle in the Delta.* Cambridge, Mass.: Harvard University Press, 2003.

Youth of the Rural Organizing and Cultural Center. *Minds Stayed on Freedom: The Civil Rights Struggle in the Rural South.* Boulder, Colo.: Westview Press, 1991.

Acknowledgments (*continued from p. iv*)

Document 9: "Warning—Citizens of Ruleville," August 27, 1964, William Heath Research Papers, 1963–1997, Box 5, Folder 14, Wisconsin Historical Society, Madison, Wisconsin.

Document 13: "Guidelines for Interviewing," 1964, Alicia Kaplow Papers, 1964–1968 Archives, Box 1, Folder 4, Main Stacks, Wisconsin Historical Society, Madison, Wisconsin.

Document 14: Civil Rights Movement Veterans, Application form for Andrew Goodman, http://www.crmvet.org/docs/64_cofo-goodman_application.pdf.

Document 15: "Security Handbook," Jerry Tecklin Papers, 1964; Archives Main Stacks, Mss 538, Box 1, Folder 5, Wisconsin Historical Society, Madison, Wisconsin.

Document 16: "Letter to Freedom School Teachers," 1964, Hank Werner Papers, Box 1, Folder 1, Wisconsin Historical Society, Madison, Wisconsin.

Document 22: "Notes on Teaching in Mississippi," 1964, Wisconsin Historical Society, Freedom Summer Collection. Memorandum to Freedom School Teachers: Overview of the Freedom Schools, http://content.wisconsinhistory.org/cdm/compoundobject /collection/p15932coll2/id/42343/show/42298/rec/1.

Document 26: Compiled from Ellen Lake Papers, 1964, Archives Main Stacks, SC 3057, State Historical Society of Wisconsin, Madison, Wisconsin, Folder 1; and William Heath Papers, Box 3, Folder 1.

Document 36: "Remarks before the Credentials Committee," August 22, 1964, William Heath Papers, Box 6, Folder 24.

Index

163

Order Form

Meriwether Publishing Ltd.
PO Box 7710
Colorado Springs CO 80933-7710
Phone: 800-937-5297 Fax: 719-594-9916
Website: www.meriwether.com

Please send me the following books:

_____ **Fifty More Professional Scenes and** $15.95
Monologs for Student Actors #BK-B267
by Garry Michael Kluger
A collection of short one- and two-person scenes

_____ **Fifty Professional Scenes for** $15.95
Student Actors #BK-B211
by Garry Michael Kluger
A collection of short two-person scenes

_____ **Audition Monologs for Student Actors** $15.95
#BK-B232
edited by Roger Ellis
Selections from contemporary plays

_____ **The Theatre Audition Book #BK-B224** $16.95
by Gerald Lee Ratliff
*Playing monologs from contemporary, modern,
period and classical plays*

_____ **Millenium Monologs #BK-B256** $15.95
edited by Gerald Lee Ratliff
95 contemporary characterizations for young actors

_____ **The Complete Audition Book for** $17.95
Young Actors #BK-B262
by Roger Ellis
A comprehensive guide to winning by enhancing acting skills

These and other fine Meriwether Publishing books are available at your local bookstore or direct from the publisher. Prices subject to change without notice. Check our website or call for current prices.

Name: _____ e-mail: _____

Organization name: _____

Address: _____

City: _____ State: _____

Zip: _____ Phone: _____

❑ **Check enclosed**

❑ **Visa / MasterCard / Discover #** _____

Signature: _____   Expiration
date: _____
(required for credit card orders)

Colorado residents: Please add 3% sales tax.
Shipping: Include $3.95 for the first book and 75¢ for each additional book ordered.

❑ *Please send me a copy of your complete catalog of books and plays.*

About the Author

Garry Kluger was born in Baltimore, Maryland, and started acting in theatre at the age of eight. Since moving to Los Angeles, he has appeared in over twenty films and television shows, many commercials, and more than fifty plays, both popular and classic.

Garry's writing includes his first two books, *Original Audition Scenes for Actors*, which won an award in 1988, and *Fifty Professional Scenes for Student Actors*. His other writings include scripts for television, movie reviews, and magazine and newspaper articles. Garry, along with his wife Lori, were the head writers for the award-winning Discovery Channel series, *The Ultimate Guide*, and Garry has written series for the FX Channel and many live shows for The Disney Company.

With all that he's written, Garry's real passion lies in his theatre work, where he has written six plays: *Till Death, Or Whatever Do Us Part* (now in print); *Office Hours; In a Yellow Wood; Brotherhood; The Homecoming*; and *Leather, Sculpture, Tourmaline, and Gold*.

The scenes from Garry's books are continuing to be used to audition actors at most of the major networks. They are also the favorite of many classes from Los Angeles to New York. Garry is very proud to be able to share his work with other actors.